MW00878863

HOW TO GET OUT OF DEBT

YOUR PERSONAL PLAN FOR DEBT ELIMINATION

BRIAN ANDERSON

CONTENTS

Brian Anderson

indirect, that are incurred as a result of the use of the information contained within this document, including, but not limited to, errors, omissions, or inaccuracies.

.

INTRODUCTION

"It doesn't matter how slow you go, as long as you do not stop."

— CONFUCIUS

Do you know how much money you owe right now?

You may vaguely remember a time in your life when you didn't have any debt. Most of us don't know the exact moment when it began to pile on, and the awareness only comes when we already have so much and no idea what to do.

If this situation sounds familiar to you, you're not

alone. I was the same way. I lived my life without worrying about debt until that fateful day when I sat down, made a list and realized that I was already drowning in financial obligations. But as I tried to remember how I got here, I couldn't pinpoint the moment when I started relying on loans, buying things that I couldn't afford and stopped thinking about how I would pay in the future. Just like most people, I fell into the alluring traps of debt and I didn't know how to get myself out.

That is until I made a choice to change my life... and you can do this too.

To give you a better idea: the average American at 35 is approximately $67,400 in debt. This is a huge number, especially when you try to think of how to pay this with regular income on top of other expenses and financial obligations they are already setting aside money for. But this value seems small compared to the amount of debt owed by Americans between 35 and 44 which is $133,100. And for those between the ages of 45 to 54, where their debts reach $134,600. Looking at these numbers, you can see a trend wherein people seem to struggle with debt payment as they age.

The fact is, the types of debts owed by people are a

reflection of where they are in their professional and personal development. This just means that generally, people adapt the same spending habits and rely on the same financial solutions when they are in a certain age group. Here is a brief look at these age groups and their financial situations:

- **35 years old and below.** Millennials, their most significant source of debt is student loans and credit card expenses. Employed individuals in this age group spend about 40% of their monthly salary on non-essential items like entertainment, clothing, gadgets, and other discretionary costs. Sometimes, some overlook setting aside money for savings because they feel like they are too young to do this.
- **36 to 44 years old.** The most significant source of debt for this range is a mortgage. Many make the choice to purchase their first home by this time. This can mean taking out a significant loan to pay off the home that usually lasts for more than 10 or 15 years. This is also when a lot of people start a family which, in turn, leads to more expenses.

- **45 to 54 years old.** Most of the time, people in this age group experience stabilization in their financial situation including debts. Some are still paying mortgages and any remaining student loans. People in this age range aren't as extravagant as those in the younger age groups and focus on saving for retirement. For those with children, their greatest source of new debt is advanced education.

- **55 to 64 years old.** Those who belong in this age group are generally paying off their debts. That is unless they take new loans for whatever purpose. Generally they are already able to focus more on building a nest egg for retirement.

- **65 years old and above.** Ideally, those who reach retirement age shouldn't have any remaining debt. While there are still those who struggle financially, those who have made the effort to save throughout their life can use this money to enjoy their free time and live their lives to the fullest. For this age group, the most common source of debt is medical bills, especially those with chronic illnesses.

As you can see, debt can reach and affect your life no matter your age. Even the richest people in the world still have some form of debt owed although they might not feel the effects of these obligations because the money continues to flow. But for the average person, at some point, we will feel the weight of debt when it gets too much.

In a 2018 survey, 23% of the people asked claimed that they didn't have any outstanding debts. In the same year, about 13% of people from a different survey believe they will continue to pay off debt for the rest of their lives. It's not just individuals who owe money to lenders—couples and families are affected too. People who decide to get married and start a family also make the choice to consolidate their debts and work together to pay everything off for their benefit.

There are so many factors that contribute to people having debts. From healthcare, housing, tuition, loans, and so much more, there are many things necessary in life that come with a steep price tag and this doesn't include the things we want. With these expenses, your income might not be able to pay for them all—and this is when you start accumulating debt. At some point, you will realize how high this number is and seem impossible to get rid of.

Don't accept debt as a part of your life. If you want to join the small percentage of people who don't own any debt whatsoever, you have to start working on it right away. To do this, taking financial responsibility is key... and this is exactly what you will be learning in this book. Here, I will provide you with all the relevant information you need along with the financial tools to help you gain a better understanding of your financial situation as a whole. Through this, you will be able to take the correct actions needed to regain your financial stability by paying off debt.

I grew up in a poor family. My mother raised me and my two siblings by working multiple jobs and making a lot of sacrifices. I still remember Christmas time when our neighbors had glittering Christmas trees with lights strung up from end to end and a house full of cheer while we had no tree, certainly no presents and no special cheer to be found. I remember my mother trying to hide her struggle from us, we didn't have time to worry about missing presents or lights but at times we did have to worry about where we would be sleeping.

Growing up in this endless struggle to stay afloat, I made a promise to myself to find the secret to financial stability so I could take better care of my family. I worked a number of odd jobs to help my mother with daily expenses while finishing my education. I enrolled in a community college and successfully applied for a low-income student grant. This was my life's turning point as it allowed me to take an undergraduate course in finance and eventually acquire my Master's Degree in Financial Engineering from Columbia University.

While I was still studying, I became an intern in a Fund Management Company. Through the years, I managed to climb the corporate ladder until I became a partner at the same company. Still, I felt like something was missing. Although I had achieved a lot in such a short time, I didn't feel professionally fulfilled. So I quit my job and started my own financial consultancy firm. Through my business initiative, I was able to work with people in desperate need of credit and financial counseling. I have helped clients from all walks of life regain their financial footing and this is how I gained the professional fulfillment I so longed for.

Still working as a financial consultant, this is my

second book that focuses on financial well-being. I know how troublesome debt can be, thus, I decided to write this specifically to help you and others like you to start the journey to becoming debt-free. My first, *The Credit Score Blueprint,* focused on regaining control of one's life by taking financial responsibility. And this is a continuation of that truth, helping you learn how to get out of debt, eliminating one of life's most significant stressors. With that being said... shall we begin?

IT'S TIME FOR A WAKE-UP CALL...
HOW BAD IS IT?

Debt refers to an obligation — typically an amount of money — that you owe to another person, bank or creditor. Just like you, many people and corporations use debts to make large purchases when they don't have enough money to afford the amount outright. When you enter a debt arrangement, you borrow money and in return, assuring repayment of the amount borrowed with interest. If you want to stop living a life in fear of debt, the first thing to do is acknowledge your current situation. If you don't want to believe that you are struggling with this, you might keep accumulating new debt. Then one day, you will be in too deep with no clear way out.

But if you make a conscious choice to accept and

understand your financial situation, then you can start making the right choices when it comes to your finances—and this is exactly what we will be discussing in this first chapter.

By far, the most common types of debt come in the form of credit card debt and loans, especially auto loans and mortgages. These days, so many people own credit cards which makes it much easier to purchase any item on a whim. After all, even if you don't have money now, as long as your credit card is in your wallet, you will be able to make purchases. Even if you didn't plan on buying anything and don't need it, a credit card can easily change your mind. For loans, you as a borrower are obligated to repay the entire loan balance by a specific date. For large loans, this usually takes several years to completely pay off. And with loans, there is always an interest rate to pay, thus, increasing the original amount of the money you have borrowed. Still, it seems like a very convenient option because it allows you to purchase things that you couldn't afford otherwise.

Looking at these common forms of debt, they represent the two main types—unsecured debt and secured. Credit card debt is a type of unsecured debt as it isn't backed by any assets as collateral. However, you still need to repay this debt at a specified date each month. Otherwise, you might face consequences such as constantly receiving calls from creditors, wage garnishment, and you can even get sued. Loans, on the other hand, are a type of secured debt because you would have to pledge a valuable asset as collateral. For an auto loan, your car is the asset. So if you can't pay on time, the creditor can repossess your car. In the same way, when you take out a mortgage and you can't pay on time, the creditor can foreclose your home. Secured debts are much harder to pay off so you should think carefully before acquiring such a debt.

No matter what type of debts you have, it's important to make a plan for how to pay them. This is the only way you can free yourself from debt and remove this huge stressor from your life. But when you try to analyze your own financial situation, ask yourself... How bad is it?

CALCULATING YOUR DEBT TO INCOME RATIO

For you to get a clearer picture of your financial situation, the first and most important thing to do is to calculate your debt-to-income ratio (DTI). Your

DTI ratio is the percentage of your monthly income that you use to pay your debts. DTI ratio isn't the same as credit utilization as this is the amount of debt relative to your credit limit lines and credit cards. Most lending institutions, especially those who offer auto loans and mortgages use the DTI ratio to determine the amount they can offer you. And they calculate this based on how much you currently spend on debts and your current income.

You don't have to wait for financial institutions to calculate your DTI ratio for you. Since your ultimate goal is to free yourself from these chains, taking proactive steps to learn all about your financial situation and doing something about it are key. Fortunately, it's easy to calculate your DTI ratio so you can figure out what percentage of your monthly income goes towards the payment of your debts. To calculate your DTI ratio, all you have to do is get the total of your monthly payments by adding up all the values then divide this total by your gross monthly income. The formula for DTI ratio is:

DTI ratio = total of monthly debts / gross monthly income

Here, your gross monthly income is the total money you earn each month before deductions. To make things clearer for you, use these steps to guide you when calculating your DTI ratio:

- First, determine the amount of money you spend on debt every month. To do this, make a list of all your financial obligations (debts) and next to those, the amounts. Some of the most common monthly debts are:
- Auto loan.
- Child support or alimony payments.
- Minimum payments for your credit cards.
- Rent or mortgage payments.
- Student loan.
- Other loans or lines of credit.

When making your list, you don't have to include things like groceries, utilities, or insurance as these aren't things you owe. To help you determine debt, keep in mind: if it doesn't show up on your credit report, you don't have to include it in your DTI ratio computation. Create your list of debts and be thorough to create an accurate value of your DTI ratio.

- The next thing is to determine your total monthly income. This is the other half of the DTI ratio, so this number also needs to be accurate. For this step, add the amounts of all your income every month from the following sources:

- Salary from your job whether you're self-employed or you work in a company.
- Overtime pay.
- Other bonuses.
- Child support or alimony payments.
- Other income that you get from different sources.
- After you get the total values of your debts and income, it's time for some simple calculations. To get your DTI ratio, divide the total of your debt payments by the total of your monthly income each month. Multiply this value by 100 to get the percentage value of your DTI ratio.

As you can see, the computation is actually quite simple. The challenging and time-consuming part is determining the values of your total debts and income, especially if you have never thought about this before. If you don't want to calculate this value manually, you can also use online DTI ratio calculators. However, you still have to find out your total debt and income values each month. After calculating your DTI, the value you get should fall into one of the following categories:

DTI of 36% and below

These values indicate a very healthy DTI that you can manage easily. If your DTI falls within this category, great! Avoid accumulating more debt to maintain this good ratio. You will find it is easier to be approved for loans once your DTI is this low.

DTI between 37 to 42%

If you fall within this category, you have a fair DTI but it's not considered optimal. In other words, your DTI is good but there is room to improve. After calculating your DTI, if you discover a value within this range, it's time to start paying off your debts.

DTI between 43 to 49%

If you fall within this category, you may already be in financial trouble. Having a DTI this high means that you should start paying your debts aggressively to keep your situation maintained. Doing this prevents you from getting into an overloaded financial situation in terms of debt.

DTI of 50% and above

Having a DTI this high should be a wake-up call for you as this ratio is extremely dangerous. This indicates that over 50% of your monthly income goes toward paying your debts. If you have this high a DTI, work on aggressively paying off your debt. Consider seeking help from a financial consultant to fix your issues.

The good news here is that your DTI ratio doesn't affect your credit score. This is because agencies that are responsible for credit reporting don't include your income when performing calculations even if they know how much you make. However, the amount of credit you use (or your credit utilization ratio) as compared to your credit limits affects your credit score. The same agencies know how much your credit limits are and financial experts recommend that you keep any credit card balance lower than 30% of your total credit limit. Despite this, it's still important for you to monitor your DTI ratio so you know if you're going into the "dangerous" ratios. If you want to get out of debt, aim for a low DTI ratio.

WHAT IS A REASONABLE AMOUNT OF DEBT?

While this is a very practical question to ask, there is no standard answer to it as it all depends on your current income, the current life stage you're in, your financial goals, your saving and spending habits, your financial responsibilities, etc. To help you figure out what is a "reasonable" amount, use these rules as a guide:

1. The 28/36 Rule

While trying to determine a reasonable amount of debt, follow the 28/36 rule. According to this, your household should only spend up to 28% of your gross income each month on mortgage, property taxes, homeowners insurance, and other home-related expenses. Then you should only spend up to 36% of gross income each month on debt. You can use the final 36% for savings and other expenditures.

This is the most common rule when calculating the reasonable amount of debt for yourself or household. Most creditors such as mortgage lenders typically use the 28/36 rule to assess a person's borrowing capacity. For this, their basis is that people who have debts above the parameters here may struggle leading to default.

Your credit score is one of the main factors considered for creditors to approve your loan or credit applications. Before they even consider approving your credit application, lenders would require you to have a credit score that falls within a reasonable range. Of course, your credit score isn't the only thing that lenders consider—they also consider your DTI ratio and income. Going back to the 28/36 rule, lenders typically use this to come up with a structure for their underwriting requirements. Then some lenders adjust the parameters based on your credit score. This allows borrowers with high credit scores to have DTI ratios that are slightly higher too.

When lenders use the 28/36 rule while assessing credit, they may also ask you questions about your comprehensive debt accounts during the application processes. Keep in mind that different lenders have their own parameters for their underwriting programs. Generally, though, they want to see that you only spend up to 28% on house-related expenses and no more than 36% on your debt payments. Since this rule is the most common one used by lenders, here's an example of computation to clear any confusion.

For instance, you earn a total of $50,000 each year and you want to follow the 28/36 rule. This means that your house-related expenses shouldn't go beyond $1,167 each month or $14,000 each year. It also means that your debt payments shouldn't go over $333 each month or $4,000 each year. This is just an example of a reasonable amount of debt based on the 28/36 rule. To apply this, make your own calculation based on how much you earn each year or each month.

2. 20/10 Rule

If you want to keep your debts in check, then you can follow the 20/10 rule. Here, your debts should only amount to 20% of your yearly income after tax deductions. This means if you earn $80,000 each year or $6,667 each month, your total debt payments should not exceed $16,000 each year or $1,333 each month. This includes all of your consumer debts.

However, the limitation of this rule is that it doesn't include your house-related expenses like rent or mortgage payments. For these payments, you can set a percentage based on how much you have left. But the 20/10 Rule is great for keeping track of your debts. If you follow this rule, you can set a limit for yourself when it comes to taking on debts. If your debts already amount to 20% of your total income, then you should reconsider taking on new debts that will push you over the limit.

To apply this rule to your finances, start with your income each month after tax deductions. Multiply this amount by 0.10 (or 10%) to get the maximum amount that you should be spending on your monthly debt payments. If you discover that you are currently paying more than this amount, then it would explain why you always seem to be struggling with your finances. To get the total amount of debt you should have, start with your yearly income after tax deductions. Then multiply this amount by 0.20 (or 20%). Your total outstanding consumer debt should be lower than the value you get from this computation.

As I have mentioned, the 20/10 rule is an excellent guide to help you avoid taking on too much. But this rule is more restrictive compared to the 28/36 rule, especially with a student loan. Typically, student loans can already place you over or close to the threshold of the 20/10 rule. If you follow this rule strictly, this means that you won't be able to take on any other consumer debts until you have completely paid it off. For many people, this proves to be extremely challenging.

Both the 26/36 rule and the 20/10 rule aren't hard and fast rules you must follow. Instead, they are guidelines that you can use to determine whether your current debts are still considered reasonable or if you are already at risk for drowning in debt. To help you determine which rule to follow, try to assess your own financial situation. If you don't have a lot of consumer debts and you haven't taken out a mortgage yet, then the 20/10 rule might be ideal. But if you have many financial obligations, you might be able to keep everything balanced better by using the 28/36 rule. Either way, use these rules to guide you towards bettering your financial situation.

SIGNS YOU MIGHT ALREADY BE IN TROUBLE

While it's easy to accumulate debt, it always comes to a point where it feels like a heavy burden that prevents you from moving freely through life. When you get to this point, it means that you are already struggling with your debt. In turn, you won't be able to get more loans, make investments, save up for a comfortable retirement, or pay for emergencies, etc. In fact, if your debts are already taking up most of your earnings, you might find it difficult to afford simple or inexpensive things. Imagine how bad you would feel when Christmas comes along and you can't afford to buy small presents for the people you love because you're struggling with debt.

Aside from not being able to afford the little things, having too much debt also has a negative effect on your credit score. And the worse your credit score is, the more you have to pay interest on loans and credit cards. Having too much debt is truly inadvisable as it traps you in a dangerous financial loop that can be very difficult to get out of. Aside from making calculations, there are signs that indicate you are already in trouble.

1. You don't have any savings

If you have been working for a long time and still don't have any money saved, this might be because your debts aren't allowing you to set aside anything extra for savings or even build your emergency fund. Unfortunately, without any savings you can accumulate more debt, especially in cases where you use your credit card to pay for essentials and in emergencies. In cases where you need money to pay for something—like if you are sick in the hospital for a few days—you would have to use your credit card to pay your medical bills since you don't have any savings or emergency funds to pay from.

Having a good amount of savings is an indication that you are managing your personal finances well. This means that you still have money to spend even if you encounter unexpected hardships or if you lose your job. Naturally, this isn't possible if all or most of your income goes to paying debt while the rest goes to other monthly expenses. Therefore, if you have zero savings, this is already an important sign that you are struggling with your debts.

2. You can only afford to pay the minimum amounts on your credit cards or loans

With credit cards and loans, expect to receive notices for these each month. But if you have too many, you might not be able to pay more than the minimum amount. With too much debt, your budget is always stretched thin, and that would only cover the minimum. But the bad news is this habit keeps you trapped even longer and ends up being more expensive as you will continue to pay shifting finance charges.

Although paying the minimum may work for you now, know that this method would take about 12 to 15 years to finish. And that is only if you stop using your credit card. If this situation sounds familiar, consider creating a spending plan. That way, you can better plan your finances and start making real progress on your credit or loan debts.

3. One of your credit cards is maxed out or near the limit

This is another common sign that you are struggling with debt. If you own a credit card, you know that it has a limit. You can't keep swiping your credit card endlessly. Be aware of your limit so you know when it's time to stop using it. With more than one credit card and one maxed out or close to being maxed out, this is a red flag. It's important to note that most credit cards charge when you reach the maximum or spend over the limit. When it comes to credit, make sure you are not spending more than 80% of your limit so you don't end up in the "danger zone."

Reconsider owning more than one credit card. When you have several credit cards, you are more likely to depend on them for spending instead of your actual income and budget.

4. Your application for new credit gets denied

The more you use your available credit, the more your credit score will go down. And when you have a low credit score, it becomes more of a challenge to consolidate your debt or apply for new credit. Therefore, if you're having trouble paying off your debt, then you can expect to get denied when you apply for new credit. The reason for this denial is that lenders only agree to lend money to those who they know will be able to pay on time. Of course, if you're struggling to pay current debts, taking on a new account will only add to your struggle and is considered fiscally irresponsible. If you want to increase your chances of getting approved when applying for a credit card, pay off existing debt first.

5. You struggle with other expenses

When you find yourself struggling to make your monthly payments—not your debts but your utility bills, insurances, and more—and you often pay these late, this is another sign that you may already be in trouble. Always paying your bills late shows that you are having trouble budgeting your monthly income. Because of this, you might end up using your credit card to pay for small purchases such as groceries, gas, and more.

Then you go back to the issue where your expenses almost reach your credit limit, thus, pushing you to struggle more. As I have mentioned earlier, it's very easy to get stuck in a loop when you're in debt. I know this because I have experienced it too. But the more you make yourself aware of the situation, the more you can take the necessary steps to improve your financial standing by getting rid of your debts gradually.

6. You don't answer calls from unknown numbers because you're worried it's a creditor

If you aren't able to pay your bills, then you can expect calls from debt collectors. Delinquent debts are usually bought by third-party collection agencies and that's when the calls start. While it's possible to avoid their calls, in the beginning, you shouldn't make this a habit.

Receiving calls from debt collectors may seem scary or even frustrating but things can get worse if you don't answer their calls. Some might go as far as suing you and if they win, they might get the permission of the court to charge your personal bank account or even garnish your pay. No matter how much trouble you're in because of debt, figure out a plan with these creditors so you don't create more issues for yourself.

7. You're starting to hide the true nature of your problem from the people you love

As your struggles become worse, you might think it's easier to hide your situation from your family or loved ones. Once you start doing this, it is a clear indication of trouble. You might feel guilty about the money you owe and you don't know how to tell your loved ones about it. Or you might feel scared about how they would react if you tell them how bad your financial situation is. No matter what the reason, hiding your struggles with debts can make things worse for you. It's better to be honest with them, especially as they might be able to help you deal with or overcome your financial struggles.

8. You are starting to develop physical symptoms because you worry excessively about your debts

When you are constantly worried about how to pay your bills, how to stretch your budget, and the consequences of not being able to pay your debts, all of these worries can start taking a toll on your body. Because of this, you may experience health issues like high blood pressure, insomnia, heartburn, anxiety, and more. This is one of the most dangerous signs of debt trouble. Think about this, if you were to fall sick, and couldn't work. How will you earn money?

Of course, if you don't earn money, you can't pay your bills, which, in turn, makes you feel even more stressed. To rid your life of panic, stress and the physical symptoms that go along with them, it's better to find a solution to the problems. Face them head-on and make a plan.

When you realize and accept that your debts are a problem, you can start thinking of ways to make things better for you. Now that you know the most common signs, you can easily recognize them if/when they are happening. If you're currently struggling, you probably recognized these situations. For now, the best thing you can do is to keep reading as there is still a lot to learn.

10 MYTHS ABOUT DEBT YOU STILL BELIEVE

Financial awareness and knowledge aren't very common, especially among the general public. A lot of people have gotten so used to living in the shadow of debt that it has become a way of life. However, this isn't ideal and comes with many disadvantages. Aside from always having to worry about stretching your income, having too much debt will make you feel like you can never catch up with your finances making it difficult to live a full, happy life.

If you're like most people who are currently struggling with debt, you might not even know how you got here. As a financial consultant, I have encountered a lot of people who found themselves drowning in debt because they believed certain money myths that hold no truth to them whatsoever. There are so many common myths and misconceptions out there and believing these can be extremely harmful to your financial health. In this chapter, we will go through these common myths, debunk them, and provide you with a more realistic explanation about the reality of this situation. That way, you can start spending more proactively and finally breathe a sigh of relief.

Paying Off Your Debt Will Repair Your Bad Credit Score Instantly

Although paying off your debts is the best possible outcome, it won't repair your bad credit score right away—it's more complicated than that. Your credit score doesn't just change at the drop of a hat. Whenever you see your credit reports, they provide you with a summary of your current standing, as well as, your credit history. This means that most of the negative information regarding your credit standing will remain in your credit report for up to seven years. If you file for Chapter 7 bankruptcy, this will remain in your credit report for up to 10 years. While paying off your debts will help improve your credit score and your overall credit report, this won't erase your history. These things take time.

When you pay off your debts, you are eliminating your obligation and taking a step towards repairing your credit. In fact, when you start paying your debts in full and on time, these transactions will show up in your credit reports, reflecting a responsible consumer. Naturally, if your payments are always late or you only pay the minimum, these transactions will also show up in your credit report. And when creditors assess your credit report, they will see this history.

In line with this myth, a lot of people also believe that when you check your credit report, it will lower your score. This is another myth. Contrary to this belief, it's actually recommended for you to check your credit report yearly. You can request this free credit report every year from one of the three national credit bureaus. If you have never checked your credit report, try it today. At least you now know that it's better to check than just hope your credit score is good. When you know your actual credit score, you can start taking the necessary steps to repair or maintain it.

- By paying all of your debts in full and on time. If you fall behind because you don't have enough, don't panic. As soon as you have the money to catch up, save it. This is the most effective way to fix a bad credit score.

- Checking your credit report thoroughly. Sometimes, you might find errors and in such a case, you can dispute them as soon as possible so that they can be rectified on record.

- Learning how to budget your income properly. After you are paying your debts regularly, the next thing is to make sure that you are only spending less than what you are earning each month.

- Avoid applying for new credit. Since you're already struggling with debt, applying for new credit cards or credit lines is a huge no-no. Even if you plan to use these to pay off your existing debts. It's better to stick with your budget than to keep applying for new loans and credit to pay off what you owe. This only makes things worse.

Also, you don't have to rely on credit repair companies to fix your credit score. No matter what these companies say, they don't have the legal right to erase negative information from your credit report.

In fact, the steps they would take are the same steps you can take on your own. So it's better to rely on yourself and be proactive to get the results you desire in terms of your credit score.

It's Okay to Only Make Minimum Payments

This is one of the more dangerous myths out there— many think that it's okay to always make minimum payments. After all, they're still making payments, right?

Wrong.

Most people make minimum payments so that they won't have to pay late fees. Also, making minimum payments doesn't have a negative impact on your credit report. However, if you want to get out of debt, it's still recommended to pay off your debt each month. If you can't do this, you can at least try to pay more than the minimum each month. Either way, you will be making a significant difference in your debts as you would be paying them off bit by bit.

Although making minimum payments isn't an issue for credit card providers, it is disadvantageous for you in the long run. This is mainly because paying off your debt this way means that it will take you a very long time to complete the whole payment which also means that you will be paying a higher amount of interest in the long-run. Let me give you an example to make things clearer for you:

For instance, let's say that your credit card balance is $5,000. Usually, the minimum monthly payment for credit card balances is 2% of the total amount with a yearly interest rate of 15%. Following this computation, your minimum payment would only be $100 a month. If you stick with this projected minimum payment, you will need approximately 24 years to pay off your debt completely—along with an interest of over $7,000. But if you try to increase the amount that you pay each month to $125 (meaning you would only add $25 to your payments per month), you can pay off your debt in five years and have over $5,000 saved in interest.

Think about how big this change is when all you have to do is add $25 to your monthly payment. Now, try to determine how much you can add to your monthly payments each month. If $25 can make a huge change, a bigger amount can make an even bigger change! It's all about learning how to budget your money and see if you can spare some money to add to your minimum payments. Even if you have to make a few adjustments here and there, you will feel better about your finances when you see your debts getting smaller and smaller.

Credit Cards Are Your Emergency Fund

Just because you have a credit card or more than one, this doesn't mean that you automatically have an emergency fund. While it's true that you can use your credit card to pay for unexpected or emergency situations, each time you do this, you are actually adding on debt. If you're already struggling with money, using your credit card every time something unexpected happens you will continue to struggle. So if you have been led to believe this myth, it's time to make a change.

When it comes to an emergency fund, the general rule of thumb is to save enough for approximately 3 to 6 months' worth of expenses. For this, you may have to do some computations and budget analysis. Try to make a list of your expenses each month and multiply this by three, four, five, and six. This total gives you a target to reach for a suitable emergency fund.

Right now, saving up such a large amount may seem like a difficult task, especially if you're already struggling financially. But when you think about it, the reason why you don't have an emergency fund already is that you were too focused on paying off your debt. With that constant mental state of making debt the priority, it can be impossible to have any lifeline in your bank account. It may be difficult, but it's not impossible.

It goes back to how you budget your income. From applying the things you have learned to what you now include in your budget this is the amount that will increase your minimum monthly debt payments and how to save for emergencies. I'm not saying fixing your budget is an easy task. But with a little bit of planning and a lot of patience, you can make the necessary adjustments to become more responsible with your finances.

While it may seem practical to cover unexpected expenses with your current income, it's better to take from your emergency fund. That way, you won't have to worry about how you're going to pay for the unplanned expense you charged on your credit card. Start building your emergency fund by setting aside part of your income until you reach your target. Remember, slow and steady wins the race. You don't have to force yourself into building your emergency fund right now, because if you don't have the money to spare now you will just see that balance go back down to $0. Stick with the plan and before you know it, you will already have a good chunk of change you can rely on when you need it.

Skipping Payments Is Normal

Despite all of your planning and budgeting, there may still be times when money is tight. If you're used to only making minimum payments each month, you might think it's not a big deal to skip a payment when faced with either paying bills or buying food. After all, you can make a bigger payment next month if you have to, right?

Wrong.

Not being able to pay the money you owe, even if it's the first time, and only once, it's a big deal. This inability to pay even the minimum should serve as a warning that something needs to change financially. For most credit obligations, skipping payments will impact your credit report in a very bad way. Although making the minimum payment isn't the best, this is still more advisable than skipping a payment completely. If you're faced with a situation where money is really tight—like if something unexpected happens, and it does, where you paid a huge sum and now you don't have enough left for your loan—try shifting your budget around a bit. Call your creditor and try to put together enough money to at least make the minimum payment on this account. This situation is common and your creditor might be able to find a way to help you out. Just be honest about the reality of your situation and come up with a better payment schedule. If this rarely happens, it might be easier for you to move your budget around to accommodate your debt.

Paying less than the minimum won't work either as this doesn't count towards the balance and is the same as non-payment. In doing this, you might have to deal with late fees, paying a higher interest rate, and this inaction showing up on your credit report reflecting negatively on your credit score.

Aside from talking to your creditor, you can also try finding ways to earn more at least until you have gotten yourself out of the tight spot you're in financially. You can try to search for short-term options to earn additional income like doing freelance work, selling some of the things you aren't using, and so on. If you're able to earn more income apart from what you're earning from your day job, you can avoid skipping payments altogether.

Collectors Will Give Up If You Stop Taking Their Calls

Have you ever experienced not answering your phone because you don't want to talk to creditors? If you remember, this is one of the signs that you're already in trouble with debt. But if you just stop answering your phone, will this make the collectors give up eventually?

No, it won't.

Although this may be partially true, this doesn't mean that the collectors will give up completely. There are only two situations where collectors will stop calling you. First, if you tell the collector that their call has come at an inconvenient time, they will probably stop calling you at that time. Second, if the collector calls you at work and you or your boss says you're not allowed to receive phone calls, they will stop calling you at work. But if you ignore the calls or tell them to stop, they don't have an obligation to legally honor such a request.

But even if you somehow manage to dodge the calls of collectors until they stop calling you, this doesn't mean that they are done. In fact, this might even make things worse. After all, collectors will only keep reaching out to you if you aren't fulfilling your financial obligations. Therefore, the best way to get these collectors off your back is by dealing with your debts or, in other words, by paying them off. As soon as you pay off all your debts, you don't have to worry about getting calls from collectors anymore.

While you aren't legally obligated to answer calls from collectors, ignoring them won't fix your problem. If you're struggling with debt, you may consider speaking to a financial consultant or even consulting with your local non-profit credit counseling agency. That way, you can learn how to come up with a plan or a way of budgeting your income to include paying off your debts. As much as possible, try not to hide from your obligations. The longer you do this, the worse your situation becomes. But if you take the necessary steps to pay off your debts, life will become so much easier for you.

You Are Only Responsible for 50% of Your Joint Debts

Many believe that getting married also means that your credit report links to your spouse creating 0ne, joint credit report or file. However, this isn't completely true. While you and your spouse will have a joint credit report, you will both still have your own individual credit reports and ratings. Apart from this, another common misconception that many believe is that once you change your last name after marriage, your credit history would get erased and you would get a new file. Convenient as this may be, especially if you know that you have a bad credit score, there is no truth to this either. Even if you get married and change your name (usually this applies to women), your credit history won't change. But it's up to you to inform creditors of a legal name change to update your file.

In general, your debts won't be merged when you get married. Although a lot of couples may agree to work together to pay off debts, neither you or your spouse are legally obligated to contribute to the payment of the other's debt. This is especially true if those debts were incurred before you got married. For instance, if you struggled with debt before getting married, this doesn't mean that you only have to pay for half of those debts after marriage. Your debts are still yours. But if your spouse volunteers to help you pay them off, that's great. The same thing goes for when you marry someone who has existing debt. You have the option to help your spouse pay off their debts even though you are not legally obligated to do so.

Of course, there is such a thing as joint credit applications. Although marriage won't link your credit files with those of your spouse, joint credit applications will create an association between you and your spouse. For instance, if you apply for a joint account or credit card or you add each other to your existing accounts, these actions will create an association between your credit reports. This is a good thing for couples who both have great credit histories but if you or your spouse has a history of bad credit, this may have an effect on each other's credit files. The trouble here is when you or your partner chooses to place your name on a promissory note for a loan or you have a joint credit account. In such a case, if you separate from your spouse and they leave without keeping up communication about finances, you could be left paying for your combined debt.

Once Divorced, You Aren't Responsible for Your Spouse's Debt

Speaking of marriages going south... the next myth many believe is that once you get divorced, you won't be responsible for your ex-spouse's debt anymore. Sadly, this is another falsehood. Even though your divorce is already final, the negative credit practices of your ex-spouse will continue appearing on your credit report once you are linked through joint accounts opened while you were still married.

Another issue is the one I shared in the last point. If you and your spouse get divorced while you have existing loans or debts in your joint accounts, you are still responsible. But if your spouse leaves without continuing payment, you will be the one responsible. Unfortunately, if those loans are too much for you to pay off alone, your credit score will plummet. For some couples, they create a separation agreement wherein they both agree to pay half of the required amount each month to pay off the joint accounts. Even if you have such an agreement in place, if your spouse doesn't make their payment, you will still be liable for the whole amount. This is because separation payments are made between spouses, not between you and the financial institution you owe. Therefore, even if you pay your share on-time and in full, if your spouse doesn't do the same, this will still harm your credit score.

The good news is that you can do something to avoid these situations from happening. If you're already having trouble with debt, adding your joint accounts will pull you down deeper. Before finalizing your divorce or separation, have a conversation with your bank or with any other lenders with which you have joint debts. Ask about the possibility of splitting your existing debts into separate loans— one for yourself and one for your spouse—to replace your joint debts. If your lender agrees to such an arrangement, good for you! At least you won't have to worry about having to pay for the whole amount while your spouse gets away scot-free.

Of course, things don't always turn out this way. Some couples keep up financial obligations even after divorce. In such a case, after you and your ex-spouse have paid off your joint debt in full, have your name removed from the account so you won't be liable in case your ex-spouse incurs debt again in the future and tries to access the same account.

All Credit is Bad

If you're struggling with debt, just hearing the word credit card will make you think of bad things. This is because the myth that all credit is bad is very common amongst young adults. But there is such a thing as "good credit" or "good debt." For this, you would borrow a certain amount of money to earn more or increase your net worth. Some things you can consider as "good debts" are loans for small businesses, mortgages, and even student loans. Although these don't come with guarantees, they are still beneficial to you financially. By no guarantees, I mean that small businesses might not prove profitable, your home may depreciate over time, and even if you have a good education that doesn't mean that you will get a high-paying job. But as long as you can afford to pay off debt without having to take out new loans, this doesn't have to be considered bad.

Since we have covered the most common debts and good debt, what are bad debts? When you depend on expensive debt like credit cards that have high-interest rates to pay for your basic expenses, then you can consider this as bad debt. Naturally, the more you use such credit and accumulate such debt, the more you will find yourself struggling to pay for everything.

Basically, debts and credit are only considered bad if you don't use them properly. But when used properly, credit is a good thing. If you don't have any credit history, then it becomes a challenge to apply for loans, mortgages, and other credit in the future. When used the right way, credit allows you to:

- Get out of emergencies when you don't have enough on hand.
- Spread out your large debts so you don't have to miss payments.
- Create a strong credit history for yourself.
- Feel safer since you don't have to carry large amounts of cash.

Just try to avoid situations that make credit a bad thing. Mainly, these situations occur when you don't understand why and when to use credit. Some examples of such situations are:

- Using your credit to purchase things that you don't need or can't afford.
- Giving in to "buy now, pay later" schemes.
- You don't completely understand the terms of the loan.
- Giving into special offers when you can't pay the debt off completely before the terms expire.

The bottom line here is that debt doesn't always have to be a bad thing. As long as you use credit correctly, you can use it to your advantage.

A Debt Management Plan Will Negatively Affect Your Credit Score

Have you ever considered creating a debt management plan? If not, it might be due to the belief that such a plan can affect your credit score negatively. But when you're faced with large amounts of debt and you don't know how to pay it off, having a debt management plan (DMP) is a very effective measure.

Many companies that offer credit counseling also offer DMPs to people struggling to pay off large amounts of debts. When you work with such companies and agree to have a DMP, they will help you negotiate with your creditors so that you can get lower monthly payments and interest rates. But when you agree to create a DMP, you need to close all of your existing credit accounts. In doing this, your credit history will get a notation to inform lenders that you have created a DMP, thus, you can't open any new credit lines. It means that you are focused on paying off your debts first. As soon as you complete your DMP or end it even before completion, the notation gets removed too.

While the notation that will appear on your credit report might make you feel worried, this shouldn't be cause for alarm. Remember that this notation is only meant to indicate that you are following a DMP. But in the long-run, it won't affect your credit score negatively. In fact, it might even improve your credit score.

For one, when you're following a DMP, your monthly debts will be automatically paid directly from your bank account. This means that your payments will always be made on time as long as you make sure that your bank account has enough money to pay off your debts. As the months go by, the timely payments will reflect on your credit report, thus, improving your credit history. After completing your DMP (it's highly recommended to complete your DMP instead of just exiting or terminating it), then you can start applying for new credit again. Doing this also allows you to continue using your credit card. But this time, you would have already paid off your debts, thus, allowing you to budget your money more effectively.

Bankruptcy is the Worst Option

Finally, we have bankruptcy—probably the scariest word you will ever encounter in the finance world. For those who don't understand what it means, bankruptcy is the worst relief option available. But the truth is, it's not. It can be your final option, but it's not the worst one. By debunking these common myths, you have already learned a number of ways to start solving debt issues. After you have considered all other options but nothing has worked for you, then you can file for bankruptcy. But you shouldn't see this as the end of the world or as a failure.

Related to this is another myth that when you file for bankruptcy, it will destroy your credit score to the point of no return and you can never have another credit line. This isn't true either. If you have reached this point, your credit score has been severely damaged and you owe a large sum. But when you add bankruptcy to the list, this won't damage your credit score as much as you might think. Despite this, you can still be approved for loans and credit lines since most lenders don't consider this as a "deal-breaker."

One reason for this is that declaring bankruptcy can help free up a percentage of your income. This will allow you to pay debts in the future. After 7 to 10 years, it will be removed from your credit history. Hopefully, by then, you would have already paid off most of your major debts and you are managing your money better.

Declaring bankruptcy isn't bad, not being able to pay off your debts is worse, especially if left unmanaged. But by reading this book, you show a strong desire to make your life better. We will be discussing bankruptcy in more detail later, but for now, I'll leave it at this: it's a relief option for those who need it.

POPULAR STRATEGIES FOR PAYING OFF DEBT

W hen it comes to paying off debt, there are certain methodologies and strategies you can use to manage your finances and achieve success in the shortest time possible. In this chapter, I will share with you the most common strategies for paying off debt. By learning these methods, you can determine the best one for your situation so you can start applying it to your life.

1. Balance transfers

This applies to when you have a large amount of credit card debt. You can talk to your bank or creditor and request a balance transfer from one credit card to another. It's practical when the balance gives you a lower interest rate. You can also do this if one of your credit cards is either nearing the limit or is already maxed out and utilizes another credit card. It's not ideal, but it is an option.

2. Paying more than the minimum amount of your credit card bills

We've already expressed that only paying the minimum balance on a credit card bill each month is a bad habit. Take a look at your current budget and see if there are any things you can move around, even a small addition to the minimum amount can shorten the total time it takes to pay off debt and it can save you in terms of interest.

3. Taking out a personal loan

You can ask different lending institutions about taking out a personal loan with a low-interest rate. This is another option for you if you have a lot of credit card bills to pay or if you have an existing credit card debt that's so large that you can't pay more than the minimum. While this alternative approach may be a smart move, you should also plan for how you will pay off the personal loan. If it involves a lower interest rate compared to the bills you're paying now, at least it might be easier to set aside payments for your personal loan from your budget.

4. Borrowing money against your life insurance

If you have life insurance that comes with a cash value, then you may consider borrowing against it. It's like you would borrow your own money. Typically, this also comes with a lower interest rate and you don't have to rush to pay it off. Still, you should work to pay off the money you owe to yourself so your beneficiary still gets the full value of your life insurance if anything happens to you.

5. Debt settlement

This option is ideal if you can afford to make a large, one-time settlement to your creditors or if you have missed the deadlines of your credit card payments. When you opt for debt settlement, you would negotiate with your credit card company or any other creditors so that they would agree to accept a set amount to settle your debt instead of paying the whole balance. However, not everyone is eligible for this option. Usually, you can qualify for debt settlement if you have recently undergone some kind of hardship in your life such as suffering from a medical condition, getting a divorce, losing your job, and the like. In such a case, you can try reaching out to your creditors to start negotiating with them.

6. Borrowing money from your 401k

You may consider this option if you participate in a 401k retirement plan. Most of these plans allow you to borrow a certain amount of money. Although the interest rates here are a bit higher than the other options I have shared, they are still lower than the interest rates of credit cards. Just like borrowing from your own life insurance, this option allows you to borrow money from yourself. Then when you pay back the amount you borrowed, it just goes back to your own account.

As you can see, there are a few options to choose from. It's all about being aware of these options and coming up with your own plan to start improving your financial situation. Now, let's take a look at the more common ways to finally rid yourself of the debt.

THE SNOWBALL DEBT PAYMENT METHOD

In a nutshell, the snowball debt payment method is a strategy that focuses on paying off your smaller debts first. When you follow this method, you would make minimum payments on all other accounts while you focus more on those with the smallest amounts. After you have paid these smaller amounts off, you start increasing payments you make on others.

The snowball method is probably the most common and well-known strategy for successfully shrinking debt, originally popularized by Dave Ramsey, an expert on personal finance. By building momentum as you pay off debt, many believe it can help you learn how to manage your finances more effectively with time.

There is a reason for the name of this method. You see, after you have paid off your smallest debt, you will still use the funds you have set aside for that payment and put those funds into your next smallest debt. In doing this, you will be "snowballing" your payments towards your next debts. And you will keep doing this until you have paid off all of your debts. Many people feel more motivated especially when they complete the payments of their debts. Even if the cleared debts are small, paying them off completely still comes with an assured sense of achievement and satisfaction. While you might still have to pay the high-interest rates of your credit card debts while following this method, it can still be a very good motivator to keep you going. If you're interested in following this method for paying off debts, here's how:

1. Check your budget

Make sure your monthly income is high enough for you to pay all the minimum amounts of your debts. To do this, make a list of all your income sources for a total. Then total the minimum amounts due. Compare both amounts to see if you have enough to cover everything. If you don't, then you can either consider a different strategy for repayment or find ways to earn more income each month.

2. Arrange your debts

The next thing to do is to arrange your debts according to the balance amount. Since you already made a list of all your debts in the last step, all you have to do now is rearrange them from the smallest to the largest. For this step, you don't have to consider interest rates yet.

3. Start paying off your smallest debt

Each month, put in a little extra money into paying off your smallest debt. Make sure you are still paying the minimum amounts on all the other debts but for your smallest debt, add more to it. Do this every month until you have paid off your smallest debt completely.

Once you have paid off your smallest debt completely, take the whole amount you set aside for that debt and add it to the payment of your next smallest debt. Again, do this every month until you have completely paid off this account.

4. Keep going it's all paid off

Repeat these steps until you start chipping away at bigger debt. It's all about using the money you have freed-up from your completed debts for the ones that are next in line. Keep doing this and you'll start seeing your debt fall by the wayside.

Pros

Following these steps you will see how simple it can be. Probably the hardest part here is to budget your money and not give in to the temptation of using newly freed-up money for anything else. Once you have paid off your smallest debt, you might feel tempted to use the "extra" money to buy things that you don't really need or even use that money to treat yourself to an expensive lunch. As much as possible, try to avoid doing this as it might derail your whole snowball payment strategy. Stick with it if you really want to see results.

There is evidence that suggests that you can potentially pay off all your debts faster this way. The snowball debt payment method can be a great fit if you have a lot of little debts to pay off. It can also be the best option for you if you think that you need the motivation to continue paying off your debts. When you have a lot to deal with, this can feel overwhelming. But the more you see yourself crossing off your debts one at a time, the more you will feel inspired to keep going. Since you will start with the smallest debt, you will see yourself progress in a very short period. Then you won't have to think about that debt anymore. As you progress, the debts you focus on grow fewer and fewer until you are only left with one or two debts to pay off, thus, making your financial situation more manageable. Naturally, when you have fewer unpaid accounts, this can help improve your credit score too.

Cons

Of course, the snowball debt payment method isn't a perfect method. Like the other strategies and methods, this one comes with a very important downside to consider. The most significant disadvantage of this method is that you might have to pay more due to interest compared to the other methods. The reason for this is that you don't consider interest rates for this method. Therefore, if your biggest loans have high-interest rates, you would have to pay for these since you will be working on paying off those loans last.

While a lot of people swear by this method, consider your own financial situation carefully before you start following it. After all, this isn't the only strategy you can use to pay off your debts. If you think that the disadvantage of this method will affect you significantly, consider other options. But if you think that this method will work and keep you motivated, go for it!

THE DEBT AVALANCHE METHOD

In a nutshell, the debt avalanche method focuses on allocating your money to making minimum payments for all of your debts. It's considered an accelerated plan for debt payment because whatever remaining money you have, you would put into your debts with the highest interest rates.

The debt avalanche method is recommended for you if you have several high-interest debts. Basically, you need to budget your income in such a way that you can make the minimum payments on all debt. Any money you have left should be added to your high-interest debts. Since you will be paying a higher amount with the highest interest rates, then you could pay off these debts first. Once you have paid off the account with the highest interest rate, keep going. When you think about it, this approach is like the opposite of the snowball debt payment method. Then you would keep paying off your debts with high interest until you have paid off all your debts. But you can only succeed in following this method if you keep with it. Otherwise, you would only be paying the minimum amounts without making significant progress.

Proponents of this method claim that it's easier to pay off your debts when you deal with the ones that are causing you the most loss—the ones with the highest interest. After creating a budget for this method, make sure to stick with it so that you can make progress in terms of paying your debts. Once you get the hang of this method, then you can start creating an avalanche. To help make things clearer for you, here's an example of how this method would work:

For instance, let's say that you have the following debts to pay along with their corresponding interest rates:

- You have a $300 hospital bill that you can pay in installments without any interest.
- You have one credit card with a balance of $5,000 and an interest rate of 15.9%.
- You have another credit card with a balance of $2,500 and an interest rate of 22.9%.

In such a situation, you would pay off the minimum amounts for all three debts. Any extra funds you have would be added to your $2,500 debt because it has the highest interest rate. After creating your budget, you can allocate your extra funds for this debt and keep doing this until you have completely paid it off. Then you would move on to your $5,000 debt before you finally focus on your $300 debt. This is just an example of how you would follow the debt avalanche method. Basically, you would just keep knocking off your debts one by one until you have paid all of them off.

There may be cases where some of your debts are under promotional interest rates. This means that they would have lower interest rates, thus, these debts probably won't be your top priority. However, if those promotional rates end, then you might have to rearrange your list of debts, especially when the interest rates go higher than the one you are currently paying off. This means that for this method, you have to keep checking all of your existing debts and their interest rates then make adjustments as needed. That way, your focus will always be on your debts with the highest interest rate.

Pros

Since this method enables you to focus on your debts with the highest interest rates, this means that you will be paying these off quicker. In the long-run, this also means that you won't have to pay high-interest rates for a longer time because you will be paying them off first. Imagine how good it would feel to see those debts disappear along with their ridiculously high-interest rates. This is why the debt avalanche method is perfect for you if you have a lot of debts with high interest rates. Think about it, if you have such debts and you use the snowball debt payment method, you will keep paying high interest until you have paid off your smaller debts first. In the long-run, this means that you would be paying more.

As long as you follow this method of paying properly and you remain consistent in terms of making payments, the debt avalanche method minimizes the amount of money you put into interest while you work towards your goals. This also helps you pay off all your debts faster since you will be getting rid of the most toxic ones first. Then you won't have to worry about interest rates accumulating over time.

Cons

For this method, the most significant downside is that you might not see progress as early as you would when you follow the snowball debt payment method. If you rely heavily on personal motivation that you get from small victories, then this method might not be the best one for you. To succeed in this method, you need commitment and discipline. Otherwise, you might get frustrated, especially if your debt with the highest interest rate also happens to be your largest amount. Naturally, this will require more time to pay.

Another potential downside of this method is that you would need enough financial resources to carry it out. If you have a lot of debts and you can't afford to pay the minimum for all of them, this means that you won't have any extra funds to put into your debt with the highest interest. Therefore, you would only be paying the minimum amounts on all of your debts which, as we have already discussed, isn't ideal. In such a case, you may have to consider another method—one that works for your own financial situation.

THE DEBT CONSOLIDATION METHOD

The debt consolidation method is another acceler-ated method for paying and it's quite popular. In a nutshell, this method involves merging several debts to create a single debt that you would pay off through a loan. For this method, you would only pay for one loan that you have taken to cover all your other debts.

The debt consolidation method is also considered a financial strategy. This is especially practical for credit card debts that have high-interest rates. When you use a loan to pay off these debts, it can help lower your monthly payments, especially if the loan has a lower interest rate too. In such a case, it becomes easier for you to pay off your debt overall. In other words, this method helps make things simpler as you won't have to deal with multiple debts and deadlines. Instead, you just have to pay one amount every month at a specific date.

While this method simplifies your debts, it doesn't get rid of your original debts. You still have to pay for them only this time, you don't pay for them separately. The main aim of this method is to reduce your obligations to a single source. There are two main forms of debt consolidation—participating in a debt management program without a loan or taking out a loan. Choose the form that suits your own financial situation best. Some people also opt to use their credit cards for this method. If you have several credit cards and you're paying them all off, you can consolidate all of your balances into a new card. This method is recommended if you find a promotional offer that charges minimal to no interest for a set time period. If you can pay everything off within that time period, then you can save money on interest rates too.

Depending on interest rates, the debt consolidation method can save you some money. However, if you can't find an option that offers a lower interest rate compared to the interest rates you pay for your individual debts, then the only advantage you would have here is the simplicity. Therefore, you should carefully consider your situation before deciding to follow this method of paying off debt.

Another potential benefit of this method is that it may help improve your credit score. If you consolidate all of your debt and find a plan that offers a lower interest rate, this enables you to make full monthly payments on time consistently. Of course, this consistency will show up in our credit report improving your score. In some cases, you might even get a tax break with this method if your debt consolidation loan is secured, for example, in a home equity loan.

If you follow this method, be careful when choosing the form of debt consolidation to use. A downside of this method is the amount of scams that exist under this name. For instance, you will be offered a lower interest rate but this gets offset by a longer period of repayment. In the long-run, this might cause you to take new loans and new debts shortly after paying off your consolidated loans. To avoid this issue, consider the payment schedules of the consolidated loans. Longer schedules mean that you would end up paying more over time. If you really want to consolidate your debts, consider how long the debt consolidated loan would last and how much you would have to pay overall. Then compare this with your current debts. While debt consolidation may be simpler, remember that your aim here is to get out of debt as soon as possible. If paying different debts at different times will help you achieve this faster, then maybe the debt consolidation method isn't right for you.

4

CUTTING EXPENSES, INCREASING INCOME, AND EVERYTHING IN BETWEEN

To get out of debt, there are two very important things you must do first—find ways to boost your income and reduce unnecessary expenditures. Of course with money, this is always easier said than done. In this chapter, you will be learning how to optimize your budget each month, how you can allocate enough to pay off your debts, and still continue living a comfortable life. Here, I will share with you a number of steps to help you regain your financial stability.

If you feel like you're treading above water in debt and you have no idea how you will manage to pay everything off, you're not alone. At some point, most will find themselves in the same position you are in right now. While living in debt seems like the "easy solution," it's not. Even if you have accepted your financial situation, deep down, you still know that you should do something to make things better. And when you start experiencing the different signs that you're struggling with debt, life might become even more difficult for you.

Yes, there are worse things than living paycheck-to-paycheck. For instance, if you keep piling on debt to the point that most of your monthly income goes into paying it off, how are you paying for everything else? Over time, the dire financial trouble you are in will take a serious toll on your body, mind, and your life.

No matter what type of debt you're struggling with, you should know that there is a way to get out of it. This change won't happen overnight and it might not be the easiest thing to do but a future free of debt is possible as long as you come up with a plan for yourself and stick with it until the end. As part of your plan, there are some basic steps you can take to change your less-than-desirable money habits and turn them around to improve your financial situation.

IT'S TIME TO START BUDGETING

Budgeting is one of the most important things you can do to make an impact on and fix your financial situation. If you don't budget your money, you don't know how much you earn, how much you actually spend, and how much you can put into paying off your debts. But once you start budgeting, you will learn. Here are a few helpful budgeting strategies to start off with:

1. List how much you earn

Write down all of your sources of income. Start with your paycheck which shows you how much you earn from your job. If you have a regular job, this should be your main source of income. If you're a freelancer or you rely on odd jobs for money, try to come up with an average amount for your monthly income. Be sure to include any other sources of income like rentals or assorted investments. Your goal for this step is to find out exactly how much you earn so you can create a budget.

2. List what you spend money on each month

Now that you know how much you earn, it's time to start working on a more realistic budget. Before you can do this, make a list of everything that you spend money on right now. It's important to be very honest with yourself when making this list. Write everything down even the most extravagant or impractical things. Creating this list allows you to see where your money goes each month and where you can make some adjustments to put towards your debts.

3. List essential expenses

With your list on-hand, create a new list but only include your essential expenses like food, utilities, rent, etc. This is important because it shows you exactly what you need to spend on and whether you are earning enough to pay for all your essentials. Apart from paying off your debts, you should be earning enough to live comfortably too. If you discover that your total income isn't enough to cover your essential expenses, how can you afford to pay off your debts too? In such a case, you may have to look for ways to earn more to help yourself out of your current financial situation.

On the other hand, you might discover that you actually have a lot more money to spare when you only spend your income on the essentials. In this case, then you can start increasing the money you put into your debts so that you can pay them off faster.

4. Compare list with essentials

This step allows you to see how much you spend on unnecessary things like new clothes, dining out, entertainment, and other luxuries. By doing this comparison, you will discover how much of your money goes into unnecessary expenses—and this is where you can start making adjustments to your budget. While you don't have to give up all of these unnecessary expenses right away, you can make another list where you arrange these expenses according to priority then cross them off one by one as you start improving your spending habits.

5. Create a new budget for yourself

With these lists you can create an entirely new budget for yourself that works. For this step, you may need time for self-reflection. Bear in mind that your main goal here is to get out of debt. So try to see where you can make changes in your current budget to make it more practical. For instance, if you discover that you spend a lot of money each month on new clothes, then this is something you may want to change. Or if you really can't stop yourself from buying new clothes, then why not consider selling those you don't use anymore? That way, you can earn extra income that you can put into buying new clothes for yourself.

This is just one example of how you can make adjustments to your budget. Think about your own situation and your own income. Then come up with a realistic budget that allows you to live comfortably and pay off your debts according to the payment strategy you have chosen for yourself. As much as possible, try to stick with the budget you have created for yourself and soon, you will start seeing your efforts pay off!

SELL STUFF YOU DON'T NEED

Speaking of selling things, this is a very effective way to declutter your home and earn some extra income with very little effort. Most people who are deep in debt often find themselves in such a situation because they like to buy things they don't need. If this situation sounds familiar to you, then it's time to make an inventory of your possessions then sell the stuff that you don't need.

Whether you live alone or with your family, you can

easily accomplish this and convince some friends they need to join in. Just take a good look around your home (or your room) and find things that have been collecting dust for years. Maybe some old books, knick-knacks or old furniture. Do you have any unused dinnerware, appliances, or even cookware to sell? Kids room full of stored linens, blankets, or old toys? For instance, do you have any old wedding or birthday presents that you haven't used since you got them? Or is your closet so full of forgotten clothes or trinkets? These are some examples of things that you can sell to earn extra cash while freeing up space in your home.

Throughout your home, you will find such items that you can put up for sale and thanks to the internet, it is very easy to sell things online through apps like Letgo or OfferUp and websites like Craigslist and eBay. You can organize a garage sale over the weekend for the people in your neighborhood to buy the things you want to get rid of and ask if any of them want to sell to make it a real event and gain more attention. Before you start selling, it's recommended to do research to find the best second hand prices for these items. If you offer quality items at competitive prices, this endeavor will be more successful for you. Also, make sure to take high-resolution photos of what you plan to sell so potential buyers can clearly see what they are buying.

The great thing about selling your stuff is that some of your possessions might turn out to be quite valuable. This is another reason why it's recommended to do research first before putting things up for sale. Through research, you can determine which of your items are of high-value and which are the ones you can sell for a cheaper price. This especially applies to toys, collectibles, and other items that typically grow in value over time.

Going back to your main goal of paying off your debts, all the money you earn from sales should go into your debts. Unless you have a more urgent need —like if you need to pay hospital bills in cash— putting this money into your debts will help you pay them off faster no matter what debt repayment strategy you have chosen.

BUDGET THE MONEY YOU MAKE WISELY

As you create your new budget, sell the stuff you don't need, and take other steps to improve your financial situation, make sure that all the money that you free up or earn goes into the payment of your debts. Don't look at it as restricting yourself. You are merely working towards a goal—to live a debt-free life. After paying off your debts, then you can use the extra money you have for building your emergency fund, adding to your savings, and even treating yourself to good food or nice things once in a while.

If you receive any bonuses throughout the year or during the holidays, part of these should go into paying your debts. Make a separate budget for these bonuses before you get them that way, you already have a plan in place. Without a budget or a plan, you might spend this money on something extravagant that you don't need or for any other luxury purchase that you might regret later on. It's important to stay focused and aware of your financial situation at all times if you want to work towards becoming debt-free.

While you follow your new budget, you should also try to adopt wiser spending habits. For instance, if you go grocery shopping, why don't you consider buying things in bulk? Instead of getting one pack of tissue papers every week, why don't you buy this essential item in bulk from warehouses and similar stores? Usually, items bought in bulk come with huge discounts. Think about the non-perishable essentials you buy regularly and try to find places in your area that sell these in bulk. As for food items, why don't you try buying meat, eggs, and produce from markets instead of grocery stores? Such items are usually sold cheaper in markets and if you buy them regularly, you'll definitely save a lot!

There are so many ways for you to save more money even when you're spending on basic, essential items. As with the previous point, you may have to do some research for this to find out where you can get discounts for buying in bulk, where you can buy fresh meat and produce for a cheaper price, where you can use coupons to get discounts, and so on. This task takes a lot of time and effort but it will definitely help improve your financial situation in the long-run.

DISCONTINUE CREDIT CARD SPENDING

This step is one of the most unpopular as most people find it extremely difficult to do. But when you think about it, credit cards will always create debt for you as they give you a false sense of wealth. For instance, if you go into a shop and you see an expensive accessory that you really want but don't need. You check your wallet and see that you don't have enough money to pay for it. But then you also see your credit card in your wallet and realize that you can buy the accessory now and pay for it later. But if you keep doing this each time you find something you want but can't afford, you will only keep creating debt for yourself.

So my next tip for you is to discontinue credit card spending and try to get in the habit of living within your means. If you find something that you like but you don't have the money for it, leave it for now. If you really want to buy that item, save up for it. After following the budget you created for yourself, if you have any money left over, put it away. Keep doing this until you have enough to buy the item that you want. Avoid the temptation of swiping your credit cards frequently by focusing on only spending the money that you have.

If you don't think that you can stop yourself from using your credit cards, take them out of your wallet and leave them at home. If you haven't built your emergency fund yet, you can leave one credit card in your wallet for emergency purposes—the one with the lowest credit limit. Even if you see promotions that offer 0% interest and you feel really tempted, remind yourself that you are trying to get yourself out of debt. Just like any other habit, breaking your credit card spending habits will take time, practice, and a lot of awareness to curb.

You shouldn't go as far as closing off your credit cards. Long-term credit can be more beneficial as it may help build your credit score. And since you have debt that you're working to pay off in a timely manner, these actions are already helping your credit score. Creating healthier spending habits for yourself will put you in a better financial situation so money doesn't have to be a struggle for you all the time.

Don't worry, though, as this will only feel like a challenge at the beginning. The more you practice spending the money that you actually have, the easier it becomes. Then you will start relying less on your credit cards while you are still working on paying off the debts you have accumulated from using them in the past. Think about your spending habits back when you didn't own any credit cards. Back then, you just used whatever money you had in your wallet and if you didn't have enough, you didn't give in to your impulses. Try to go back to that habit for the sake of your financial health.

RENEGOTIATE TERMS AND CONDITIONS

If you have been a loyal client of a certain financial institution like a bank for some time now, you might be eligible to renegotiate the terms and conditions of your credit cards, loans, and other bills. One of the biggest issues when it comes to credit cards is the high-interest rates. Sometimes, these interest rates are so high that it feels like you aren't even making a dent, other than in your wallet, in your total bill even if you pay regularly each month. If this is a problem that you have, you may want to try and reach out to your creditor. Requesting lower interest rates is quite common. As long as you have a good history with timely payments, this has a likelihood of success.

Apart from asking for lower interest rates on your credit card debt, there are other bills that you can negotiate the terms and conditions with too. Some of your fixed expenses might even fall under this category so why not try reaching out? After all, the worst thing that could happen is the denial of your request. But if you successfully negotiated a majority of your debts and bills, just think about how much you can save!

Although this strategy might seem like a long-shot, requesting lower interest rates usually leads to an improvement in the terms and conditions that you are currently following. The key here is to reach out and give it a try.

STOP CREATING MORE DEBT

Think about this: as you are trying to pay off your debts, will you be able to do this if you keep creating new money pits? If you are working to pay off your credit card, how will that happen if you continue to use it?

Another way to do this is by sticking to the new budget you created. You have put in a lot of time and effort into analyzing your current spending habits and creating a budget that's better suited for your spending habits. If you want to reach your financial goal, make sure to stick with it no matter how challenging it gets. Instead of creating new debt, focus on setting money aside for your emergency fund.

During this period of paying off your debt, focus more on saving and paying what you owe instead of spending. If you have any extra money, put it towards your savings as well as reducing credit accounts. No matter how small those extra amounts are, as long as you use them wisely, you will see your situation improving as time goes by. Living a debt-free life involves changing your current habits. After all, you wouldn't be struggling in debt right now if you had the proper habits, right?

Be patient and take a break from financial stress from time to time. Don't be too hard on yourself and the choices you made in the past. Changing your habits is a process that takes time and effort for it to be successful. Just stick with your choice to make a difference and actively find ways to motivate your-self along the way. That means making conscious choices and decisions when it comes to your finances. And when you're able to reach significant milestones, reward yourself for these. Treat yourself to something you really want but this time, make sure that you can afford it. The more you approach these steps with positivity, the easier they become. Then you can start dealing with the more serious side of debt management that we will go over now.

5

FORECLOSURES, REPOSSESSION, WAGE GARNISHMENT, AND COLLECTION EFFORTS

When you fall behind on your payments and do your best to avoid creditors, they can resort to drastic measures like foreclosing your home, repossessing property, garnishing your wages, and other collection efforts that will make life harder for you. When faced with such situations, you may want to consider an even more all-encompassing strategy to maintain your quality of life while you deal with the debt you have accumulated over the years.

Debt collectors and creditors have different strategies for collecting debts and loans owed by debtors. They may send collection letters or they may try calling you. If these simple strategies don't work, they won't just give up. After all, it is their job to collect and they will find ways to do this. You should know what other things creditors can do to ensure that you pay your debts so that you can take steps to prevent these from happening. Of course, the best thing to do is to pay off your debts but this isn't always possible. So in this chapter, we will go through the special circumstances you might face when creditors take drastic measures along with some practical and effective tips for dealing with such situations. By learning these things, you can keep yourself protected and avoid losing more than you need to because of debt.

WHAT TO DO WHEN FACED WITH FORECLOSURES

When you are faced with a threat of foreclosure, you might feel overwhelmed and panicky. After all, the idea of losing your home is anyone's nightmare. But when you receive a Notice of Delinquency, this doesn't mean you are out of options. This notice is sent due to missed payments and as a drastic measure by the creditor to get your attention. The good news is, there are steps you can take to slow the process down or even stop it from continuing.

When you purchase a home, you will sign a mortgage. This is an agreement to pay back the loan for the house according to the terms and conditions stated in your agreement imposed by the bank or creditor. Of course, when you aren't able to make payments on your mortgage, this is considered a breach of contract. And if it continues, the lender has the legal right to recoup the investment by taking the home, known as foreclosure.

Making one late payment on your mortgage isn't a cause for alarm. Ideally, you should be making these payments regularly but if you're a couple of days late, you won't be facing foreclosure right away. Typically, lending institutions would give you a grace period—about 15 days—to make your payment along with a late fee. But if you aren't able to make your mortgage payment consistently for 90 days, then the foreclosure process will begin. Fortunately, this is a very long process which means that you still have time to get back on track so you won't lose your home.

If you receive a letter from your lender about your missed payments, don't ignore them. Don't ignore calls from creditors either. When it comes to your home (and any other significant debt), the best thing you can do is be in contact with collectors, keeping communication lines open and making a deal that works for both parties. When faced with a notice of foreclosure, here are some things you can do to slow the process:

Reach out to your lender

Most of the time, lenders prefer to work directly with clients instead of dealing with the process of foreclosure. Not only is it long, but it is very costly. Therefore, if you're having trouble making mortgage payments, you can reach out to your lender and discuss what you can do in this stage. There are many options still available to you and discussing them with your lender can make things easier for both of you.

Consider refinancing

This is a process where your lender will offer you a new loan that comes with a new set of terms, conditions, and interest rates. This loan is meant to cover all of the payments you have missed along with the remaining balance that you owe. A lot of people opt to refinance because it won't harm your credit score and even decrease your monthly payments.

Come up with a new plan for repayment

For this option, you work together with your lender to come up with a plan that fits into your budget. Essentially, you will start over in terms of making payments. You will continue working to make payments over time as you also try to make up for any missed payments.

Ask for forbearance

When you request forbearance from your lender and they agree, this means that they will suspend your mortgage payments temporarily for an agreed-upon period. This can give you time to manage your finances better so that when the suspension ends, you can continue making your payments without delay. Of course, you would still have to pay the whole amount for you to own the home legally.

Ask about the possibility of loan modification

A loan modification is where your lender agrees to make modifications to your existing loan in terms of length, interest rate, and amount due. This is an excellent option for making your monthly payments more manageable for you. It can also help delay the process of foreclosure as you will already have the capacity to make full payments, especially if the monthly payment amount has decreased. However, this may also mean a higher interest rate and a longer time to pay the whole amount.

File for bankruptcy

Yes, bankruptcy is another option to delay foreclosure. When you file for bankruptcy, the process of foreclosure will immediately be suspended. For this option, it's recommended to consult with a lawyer and ask for a comprehensive explanation of the process of filing for bankruptcy to delay foreclosure along with all of the costs, the time involved, and your other options. While this step can delay foreclosure because of the suspension, it won't put a stop to the process permanently.

It's good to mentally prepare, do your research and take into consideration that filing for bankruptcy will have a negative effect on your credit score. Therefore, this should be your last option when faced with foreclosure. As soon as you file for bankruptcy, an "automatic stay" takes effect. This serves as an injunction that will prohibit your lender from foreclosing your home or even from trying to collect payments from you. This also means that all activities related to the process of foreclosure must stop throughout the process of bankruptcy. After filing from bankruptcy, you could have at least one to two months to deal with your financial issues before the process of foreclosure resumes.

There are different types of bankruptcy you can file (we'll discuss these in more detail later) but in this case, Chapter 13 bankruptcy is recommended as it allows you to keep your home. You can do this by restructuring all of your debts. This means that you would repay some of your debts in full while others in part through a repayment plan and within a set period. This option can help you avoid foreclosure while still keeping your home as you can repay your late or missed payments through the new payment plan.

Consider selling your home through a short sale

Finally, if you think that you have no other way to repay your mortgage, then you may consider a short sale. Before doing this, ask permission from your lender because a short sale involves selling your home for less than it's worth. Also, your lender will be the one to choose who to sell your home too. Communicate with your lender and talk to them about the possibility of a short sale. While this option will hurt your credit, it's better than having a foreclosure on your report.

Consult with a lawyer to ask if you're eligible for filing a lawsuit

In some cases, you may be eligible for filing a lawsuit to stop the foreclosure. But you can only know this by consulting with a lawyer. This is a possible option for you if your lender is using a non-judicial foreclosure process. This means that your lender is completing the process outside of the court system. If you can prove this, then you can file a lawsuit to stop or delay the process of foreclosure. This step is quite complex which is why it's best to consult with a lawyer first to get all the information you need along with the legal advice to go through the whole process of filing a lawsuit.

HOW TO HANDLE REPOSSESSION

The most common situation where you might face repossession is when you aren't able to make payments on your car loan. In such a case, your lender might repossess your car until you rectify your late payments. To avoid such a situation from happening, you need to resolve your debts as soon as possible. As with foreclosure, you have several options to deal with repossession. I will be sharing these options to you and your job is to determine which option is right for you when faced with the threat of repossession.

Refinance your loan

Since repossession commonly happens when you cannot make payments on your car loan, you may consider refinancing. Reach out to your lender and ask about refinancing your car loan to give you a longer-term to pay what you owe. But if you're thinking about refinancing, here are some things you may want to consider:

- If you need to make an upfront payment for the refinancing.
- The fact that cars depreciate rapidly. Therefore, you should consider whether refinancing is worth it, especially if your car is already quite old.
- If the interest rate on the refinanced loan is lower than the interest rate of your original loan. Otherwise, you might end up paying more each month after refinancing.
- If there are any other costs involved like fees or penalties.

Negotiate with your creditor

It's always a good idea to communicate openly with your creditor about your situation. Reach out and try to negotiate with your creditor to avoid repossession. For instance, you can ask your creditor if it's possible to spread out your late payments over a longer period if you don't have the full amount now. You can also consider surrendering your car to settle the deficiency. Do this if you think that you really cannot pay the balance and your car has become more of a liability. Just make sure that you get this agreement in writing to avoid any issues.

Have your loan reinstated

Reinstating your loan can either prevent repossession or allow you to get back your car if it has already been repossessed. To reinstate your loan, you can make a lump sum payment to your creditor to make up for all of your late or missed payments. Before you consider this option, check your state laws as some states don't provide the right to reinstate a car loan. However, even if your state doesn't allow you to do this, you can also check your car loan agreement as it might have a clause that allows reinstatement. Also, remember that loan reinstatement is a one-time thing. If you can successfully pull this off, make sure that you don't default again as this option will already be off the table.

Consider selling your car

Another option for you to consider is to sell your car to someone who can pay you more than what you owe to your creditor. This is a better option compared to having your creditor sell the car for you to a private dealer or a public auction. Typically, such sales won't give you enough to pay off your debt. But if you decide to sell the car yourself to a buyer who is willing to pay a good price for it, this means that you can pay off your whole debt after the sale. If you choose to do this, bring your creditor in the loop as well. This will make it easier for you to sell your car to the highest bidder.

Whatever you do, don't try to hide

Since you have several options available in terms of handling repossession, one thing you should never try to do is conceal the vehicle. If you make things difficult for your creditor, you are also making things more difficult—and more expensive—for yourself in the long-run.

Even if you try to hide your car, repo men have the legal right to come into your property and seize it.

Although the laws may vary in each state, most permit repo officials to seize cars and other possessions as long as they don't use physical force or threatening language. But there is a catch where they aren't allowed to break into a storage facility (check your facilities policy) or your garage to seize property. If you try hiding your car from these people, your creditors might charge you for the cost of hiring professionals even if they are unsuccessful in their pursuit to seize.

Even if you can successfully hide your car from repossession for some time, your creditors might take things further by pursuing legal action against you. In such a case, your refusal to turn your car over willingly means that you are violating a court order. Then the next time repo men come to your home, they can already bring with them an officer of the law to enforce the order of the court.

If you are struggling with financial issues, it's best to speak with your creditor or lender about them. Most creditors and lenders are more willing to work with their clients to deal with such issues instead of chasing after clients and their possessions. If you know that your financial issues won't run into the long-term, you can request to lower payments and resume the minimum after improving your financial situation. If you have always been a superior customer, making timely payments from the beginning and this is the first time you have faltered, your lender will likely agree to this arrangement.

However, if you're dealing with long-term financial issues, then you may consider the options we have discussed above. If you're drowning in debt and you really can't make the payments for your car, consider letting it go. After paying off your debts, you may consider taking out another car loan but this time, you would be more financially prepared for it.

It's also important to note that after repossession, you might still be able to get your car back through the right of redemption. To do this, you have to pay the remaining balance of the car loan to get your car back. However, this is quite a significant amount as it includes the outstanding loan balance, the interest, the storage cost, repo fees, and even lawyer fees. Also, after repossession, your car might be put up for auction. As soon as your car gets sold, you lose the right of redemption.

When it comes to repossession, consider all factors carefully. You may not want to let go of your car or any other material possession but if it will take a load off your finances, repossession might be your only option. The bright side here is that as long as you keep working to pay off your debts, there will come a time when you can actually afford to take out a loan for a new car without placing strain on your finances.

WAGE GARNISHMENT

Another issue you might have to go through when you try to evade creditors and debt collectors is wage garnishment. This happens when your employer receives an order from the court to take a percentage of your salary and send it to your creditor directly. Generally, wage garnishment will continue happening until you have resolved the debt or paid it in full.

Usually, creditors would resort to wage garnishment when they cannot reach you or get a response from you through calls or letters. When your creditor sues you and wins, wage garnishment takes place. The same thing may happen when you don't appear in court and in such a case, your creditor wins a default judgment. After either of these scenarios, you and your employer will receive a notice in the mail to inform you about the wage garnishment.

Wage garnishment is quite common and it's nothing to feel embarrassed about. Even if your employer finds out that you got sued over a debt, think of it this way: your employer also sees you are at least paying off your debt through this process. To avoid feeling awkward when faced with the possibility of wage garnishment, talk to your employer or someone in the HR department and inform them about your debts and what the next step would be. That way, they aren't surprised when they receive the notice. At least when the news comes from you first, it shows that you are taking responsibility and trying to improve your financial situation.

After your employer receives the notice about wage garnishment, this process will start. Usually, it would take between 5 to 30 business days for the wage garnishment to take effect. Then it will continue until you have paid your debt in full or you have found some other way to resolve your debts. There are times, though, that interest and court fees can be added to the total amount to be deducted from your wages.

While wage garnishment is a relatively simple process, there may be cases where your salary gets deducted without notification or court order. Such a case might happen if you have any back taxes, child support payments that you didn't make or any federal student loans that you haven't paid back yet. When it comes to financial issues, bankruptcy isn't the only solution and this also applies to wage garnishment. When faced with the possibility of wage garnishment, you have several options to choose from. These include:

Respond to the wage garnishment letter

Once you receive the notice of wage garnishment, reach out to your creditor right away. Since you would receive such a notice first before the wage garnishment starts, you may still have time to resolve the situation. Never ignore such a letter. If you don't want your debt payments to be deducted from your wages, call your creditor and try to negotiate a payment plan before the wage garnishment process begins.

Consider state-specific remedies

Some states offer additional protection against wage garnishment. Check the laws in your state to see if such protection exists. For instance, if you live in Ohio, you can get a request from the court for a trustee to be appointed. In such an arrangement, you can make your payments to the appointed trustee who, in turn, distributes the payments to all of your creditors. As long as the trusteeship exists, wage garnishment cannot occur. Another example is if you live in California, you have the option to make an exemption claim. For this, you can either eliminate or reduce the wage garnishment as long as you can prove that you need your whole salary for supporting your family or you are undergoing economic hardship. If your state has any of these remedies, you may consider them before moving on to the other options.

Legally object to the wage garnishment

Before objecting to the wage garnishment, you should hire a lawyer to help you throughout this process. As soon as you receive the notice, you should file an objection with the court in writing and for a hearing. You can either sign forms to request a hearing or file on your own. Here are some situations where you can object to the wage garnishment:

If you already paid off your creditor

If you receive a notice of wage garnishment after

paying your creditor partially or in full, you can object to the notice.

If your creditor neglected to follow correct procedures

Check to make sure that your creditor followed the correct procedures for wage garnishment. If you believe your creditor didn't follow standard protocol —like if they didn't give you a timely wage garnishment notice—then you can object to the notice. If you can prove your position, the court will probably terminate the wage garnishment order.

If your creditor takes too much

Of course, if your creditor takes too much from your wages, you can object to this too. Under federal law, creditors can only take your gross pay less the mandatory deductions and taxes less 30x the federal minimum wage or 25% of your gross pay less the mandatory deductions and taxes. But if your wages are being garnished for alimony or child support, then as much as 50% to 60% of your gross pay less the mandatory deductions and taxes can be garnished.

The amount of your wage garnishment would depend on the reason or the type of debt. But if you think your creditor is garnishing more than what state or federal laws allow, you may object to the wage garnishment right away.

File for bankruptcy

Finally, a last result can be to file for bankruptcy and immediately halt wage garnishment. For wage garnishment, the recommended type of bankruptcy to file is Chapter 7. When you file for this type of bankruptcy, the law will automatically impose an "automatic stay" which protects you from creditors. The automatic stay prohibits your creditors from garnishing your wages or taking any other collections from you throughout your bankruptcy.

However, there are some exceptions to the prohibition of the automatic stay. For instance, if your wages are garnished to pay child support, these will continue despite your bankruptcy case. While creditors can request the court to lift your bankruptcy case, it is highly unlikely that the court will agree unless:

- Your creditor will lose a lot of money if they have to wait for your bankruptcy to end.
- Your debt is secured by your car, your house or some other collateral.

To stop the wage garnishment, you can either provide the court with a complete list of your creditors along with their addresses. Or you can also send copies of your bankruptcy filing to your creditors if you want to speed the process along.

DEALING WITH AGGRESSIVE DEBT COLLECTION EFFORTS

When you experience financial troubles, it can be a stressful time for you. And these financial troubles often come in the form of debt. We are all familiar with calls coming from debt collectors and we all know how frustrating these can be, especially if they just keep calling. But when the debt collection efforts start getting aggressive, you should learn how to protect yourself. The good news is, there are things you can do to deal with such issues:

Know your rights

You should know that there are certain types of attempts or activities to reach out to you that aren't acceptable. These can even be considered harassment. By federal law, debt collectors are required to follow the Fair Debt Collection Practices Act (FDCPA) which dictates what they are and aren't allowed to do when collecting debts. Here are some of the most common rules debt collectors must follow as per the FDCPA:

- Debt collectors are required to identify themselves at the very start of the call.
- Debt collectors should inform you that the purpose of the call is to collect on a debt.
- Debt collectors should provide you with the complete name and address of the creditor you owe a debt to.
- Debt collectors should provide you with verification about the debt they're calling about. If you request verification, the debt collector should mail it to you within 30 days or stop calling you altogether. It's important for debt collectors to send the verification request through certified mail with a request for a return receipt. This will also serve as proof of the correspondence in case any legal issues arise in the future.
- Debt collectors should inform you of your right to partially or completely dispute the debt with them.

These are some of the most common and basic rules

that debt collectors have to follow. Naturally, there are also things that debt collectors shouldn't be doing as per the FDCPA including:

- Debt collectors cannot call you about debts you don't owe.
- Debt collectors cannot talk to anyone else about your debts.
- Debt collectors cannot call at unreasonable hours. This means that they can only call you between 8 a.m. and 9 p.m. to discuss money owed.
- Debt collectors shouldn't call you at your place of work after you have informed them that these calls aren't allowed.
- Debt collectors shouldn't call you continuously or repeatedly with the intent to harass, annoy or abuse you.
- Debt collectors shouldn't continue calling you if you have already sent a written request to stop calling. They should also stop calling you if you indicate in your written request that you don't want to pay the debt.
- Debt collectors shouldn't call you if you have hired a lawyer to represent you.

- Debt collectors shouldn't call you after you've filed for bankruptcy.
- Debt collectors shouldn't deceive you by misrepresenting themselves to make their collection efforts more effective.

As you can see, there are many rules debt collectors must follow when communicating with you about your debts. For a complete list of all these rules, you can go to the FDCPA site to find out more. It's important to know your rights as a consumer so you know when they are crossing the line.

Send an official letter that requests your creditor to stop harassing you

If you feel like a debt collector is already harassing you, the first thing you must do is send an official letter requesting them to stop. Under the FDCPA, after receiving this letter, the debt collector must stop calling you immediately. If you plan to take this step, make sure to document any harassment or illegal behavior of the debt collector. That way, you have proof to show when writing your letter. But you should only do this if you feel like the debt collector is being unreasonable or they are starting to harass you. But if the debt collector is following all the rules of the FDCPA, then it's best to deal with the situation instead of finding ways to get out of it.

File a complaint with the Federal Trade Commission (FTC)

For this step, you can request a form from the FTC to use for your complaint. You also have the option to write the letter yourself. Either way, include the name of the debt collector, the debt collector's agency, their business address, the name of your creditor, and dates and times when the debt collector called you, any names of witnesses, and a list of your complaints. If you have proof like recorded conversations, written communication, and the like, include these with your complaint letter too.

Apart from sending a complaint to the FTC, It's also a good idea to file a complaint with the debt collector's agency. Send the same complaint letter to this agency, as well as, the agency of your creditor. Sometimes, debt collectors might even offer the cancellation of your debt in exchange for withdrawing your complaint. Such an outcome would be good news for you as the harassment would come to an end along with your debt. But this doesn't always happen.

If you want to take things further, you can even choose to sue a debt collector who harasses you. But you should only do this if you know that you have a very strong case against the debt collector not just because their calls irritate you. Make sure you have all the evidence you need and you can win the case, otherwise, you would have to pay the lawyer's fees of the debt collector along with any other court costs.

File for bankruptcy

Filing for bankruptcy can also get you out of a situation where you're experiencing harassment from debt collectors. While this might be a difficult decision, it will halt any communication from debt collectors. As soon as debt collectors receive word about your bankruptcy, they should stop calling you. If you are still contacted after you file for bankruptcy, this means that the debt collector has already violated the FDCPA's bankruptcy code. In such a case, contact a consumer rights or bankruptcy lawyer right away. But remember this should be considered as a last option as it does come with consequences.

6

IS BANKRUPTCY THE ANSWER?

Throughout this book, I have frequently mentioned filing for bankruptcy as a strategy for debt management. But when you come to the point where bankruptcy is a real option, it's normal to feel overwhelmed or hesitate to file as it is a very scary concept. However, there are times when filing for bankruptcy is your best chance at financial freedom if you want to finally get out of debt and jump start your bank account.

Bankruptcy is a legal process meant to help people get a fresh start on their finances either by making a new arrangement to pay an unmanageable amount owed or erasing it completely. Some companies use bankruptcy to liquidate their assets and close in an organized manner. For most people who file bankruptcy, the most desirable outcome is a discharge. This means that creditors will be prohibited to collect debts against you permanently. However, there are some exemptions to this including alimony, child support, and tax debts.

We have already gone through situations where you would file for bankruptcy as a last resort. Usually, though, you would do this when your debts are far larger than your income and you can't seem to get ahead no matter what strategy you incorporate. Since you have learned a little about bankruptcy in the previous chapters, here is where we apply a comprehensive understanding of this process and what to expect.

THE DIFFERENT TYPES OF BANKRUPTCY

After understanding the textbook definition of bankruptcy, the next step is learning the many different types. Knowing this will help you determine which type to file. Bankruptcy is a complex process and the process of filing may vary from one state to another. But the good news is that each type —or chapter—of bankruptcy follows a basic process and uses the same basic terminology.

When filing, you and your creditor(s) are the parties involved in the process. As a debtor, you can either incur unsecured or secured debt. Unsecured debt is a debt that isn't tied or linked to any of your personal property. By contrast, a secured debt is a debt tied or linked to one of your personal properties like your car or house, for example. When creating a bankruptcy settlement, you would always start by paying off your secured debts. But before you reach this point, you should first determine what type of bankruptcy to file:

1. Chapter 7 Bankruptcy

Chapter 7 bankruptcy is also known as straight bankruptcy or liquidation and this also happens to be the most common type of bankruptcy filed by individuals. When you file for chapter 7 bankruptcy, the court will appoint a trustee to oversee the sale (or liquidation) of your property (your assets) so you have money to pay off your debts. Typically, filing for chapter 7 bankruptcy also erases your unsecured debt like hospital or credit card bills. However, you cannot file for chapter 7 bankruptcy to stop paying for your taxes, student loans or child support.

The rules on the assets that the court will force you to sell may vary from one state to another. For instance, you may still keep your basic assets like your home, your car or even your retirement account when you file for chapter 7 bankruptcy but there are no guarantees. Also, filing for this type of bankruptcy may postpone a foreclosure but not stop it from happening. If you really want to keep your assets, you have to continue with your payments like in the case of a mortgage. Chapter 7 may postpone the foreclosure of your home but after a set period, you should be able to continue paying your mortgage, otherwise, the process of foreclosure might continue.

If the court decides that your debts are too high compared to your income, this is when you can file for chapter 7 bankruptcy. For this, the court may conduct a means test where your income will be compared to your debts. If you don't earn enough money to pay off your debts, then you should qualify for filing. If you decide to go through with it, then you would need to meet with each lender and creditor to discuss your finances. Chapter 7 bankruptcy also remains in your credit report for up to 10 years and once you file for this type of bankruptcy, you have to wait for eight years before you can file for it again.

2. Chapter 9 Bankruptcy

Chapter 9 bankruptcy can be filed by cities, towns, school districts, etc. This involves the creation of a repayment plan that makes it easier for them to reorganize their finances so they can pay off their debts.

3. Chapter 11 Bankruptcy

Chapter 11 bankruptcy is the most complicated type of bankruptcy to file which means that only people or businesses who are experiencing extreme financial issues file for it. When you file for chapter 11 bankruptcy, you can keep all of your assets while you try to come up with a reorganization plan to pay off your debts. Since the creation of the Bankruptcy Abuse Prevention and Consumer Protection Act in 2005, you only have up to 120 days to work out this reorganization plan. If you cannot submit a plan after 120 days, your creditors will be the ones to submit reorganization plans that you have to follow.

4. Chapter 12 Bankruptcy

Chapter 12 bankruptcy is only for owners of farms. For this bankruptcy, the farm owner gets to keep and manage their assets while working out a repayment plan together with their creditors.

5. Chapter 13 Bankruptcy

Chapter 13 bankruptcy involves the restructuring of your current plan so you can pay off debts within 3 to 5 years. After this period, any remaining debts will be discharged. After filing for a chapter 13 bankruptcy, the court will approve your restructured payment plan allowing you to pay back part of your unsecured debts, as well as, your secured debts. The amount you have to pay each month would depend on how much debt you owe and how much money you earn in total. Also, you would have to follow a very strict budget that has been set by the court. The court will also be checking how you spend your money so you should make sure that you follow the budget.

When you file for this type, you get to keep all of your assets while you work to pay off your debts. Like chapter 7, a chapter 13 filing can also bring the process of foreclosure to a halt, thus, allowing you to update your mortgage payments. If you have unsecured debts amounting to less than $419,275 and secured debts amounting to less than $1,257,850.3, you can file for this type of bankruptcy. Another requirement for this is that your tax filings should be updated. Take note that this type of bankruptcy will remain in your credit report for 7 years and you need to wait for 2 more years before filing for chapter 13 bankruptcy again.

6. Chapter 15 Bankruptcy

Chapter 15 bankruptcy involves international issues. This type provides access to foreign debtors to the bankruptcy courts in the US.

WHEN IS IT A GOOD TIME TO FILE?

While filing for bankruptcy is a possible option to help you get out of debt, its effect on your credit doesn't just have an impact on your finances. In some cases, it might even make it more challenging for you to get insurance, apply for a job, purchase a home or rent an apartment. Generally, most people have a negative perception of bankruptcy and when you're already struggling with debt, the mere thought of filing for bankruptcy might make you feel worse about your situation.

But if bankruptcy is such a bad thing, then why does it exist?

It is seen as the last option for people who need debt relief. While you shouldn't take this process lightly, you may consider filing for bankruptcy if you are in too deep and you don't have any way to repay it— and you have run out of options. After making the choice to file for bankruptcy, then you need to think about what type of bankruptcy to file and how to go about the process. Filing for bankruptcy is a good plan if/when you meet the following criteria:

If you are threatened with foreclosure, repossession or wage garnishment, this usually means your credit score has dropped significantly. Therefore, filing for bankruptcy won't really make a difference on your current credit score. After your debt is discharged, you would have the chance to start fresh and work on improving your credit score by adopting better financial habits and practices.

Filing for bankruptcy is also a good idea if you're fed up with aggressive notices, calls, and collection activities from debt collectors. When you have to deal with these notices over time they can start taking a toll on your life, making it difficult to live normally. Since bankruptcy will prohibit debt collectors from communicating with you, this is another plus.

If you mostly have unsecured debts to deal with and you can't seem to pay them off, then you may consider filing for bankruptcy too since this can free you of such debts. Even if you have secured debts, you may still file for bankruptcy. But the difference is, those secured debts will still exist even if your unsecured debts may get discharged. It's probably best for you to make a list of all your debts first to find out which ones are secured and which ones aren't. That way, you can determine if bankruptcy is the right move for you.

When you don't have quick cash to use for paying off your debts, then you are considered insolvent. This means that your debt liabilities have already exceeded the fair market value of your total assets. This also means that you have spent so much of your money that you don't have enough left to make payments. When you're insolvent, this is a significant indicator that bankruptcy might be your best option.

Huge student loan or medical debt can take a long time to pay off and if you can't deal with them anymore, filing for bankruptcy might be a good idea. This is especially true if you keep accruing penalties and late fees because you don't have the money to pay for everything. Although bankruptcy will remain in your credit history for a long time, you would at least be getting rid of some debts that you just can't afford to pay anymore.

Nobody wants to get sued for not being able to pay off debts, right? But when debt collectors just can't get you to pay what you owe, they might resort to filing a lawsuit against you. In such a case, your only way out might be to file for bankruptcy. Just make sure to consider all of your options first before you take this equally drastic step to get out o a lawsuit.

Part of this process is to assess your current financial situation. Be honest with your assessment so that you can see what your finances really look like. After conducting your self-assessment, you might discover that your financial issues aren't temporary. For instance, if you have already considered all other options and none of them seem to apply to you, then bankruptcy might be the best step for you to take. If you're struggling with your debts, it would be virtually impossible for you to find an easy solution. Living a debt-free life isn't going to be easy and the deeper you are in debt, the more difficult it will be to get out of it. And when all else fails, this would be the best time for you to file for bankruptcy and use this as a stepping stone to improve your financial situation.

On the other hand, if you are only going through a temporary financial hardship, you may want to wait until things go back to normal before filing for bankruptcy. It's all about being honest with yourself to determine what is the best thing for you to do.

THE CONSEQUENCES OF FILING BANKRUPTCY

Filing for bankruptcy can be a powerful solution for your financial woes. Doing this can prevent a lot of collection actions from happening and it can also help eliminate some of your debts. However, bankruptcy won't solve all of your financial problems nor will it eliminate all of your obligations.

While the negative effect on your credit score might not be that significant, it will still happen. And remember that this particular action will remain in your credit history for years to come. This means that throughout those years, creditors will see that you have filed for bankruptcy at some point which conveys money management issues in the past.

Also, after filing for bankruptcy, your new credit limits will most likely be lower than they were prior to your filing. It will take years for you to recover from this but at least, you would already be on your way towards fixing your past issues with debt.

Another adverse effect of filing for bankruptcy may happen when you try to apply for loans in the future. Since bankruptcy would appear on your credit report, this might make it more difficult for you to qualify for such loans. For the same reason, applying for a new credit card might be more difficult too. When considering applicants for new credit, creditors will always refer to credit reports and credit scores. And if there is something as significant as a bankruptcy filing on it, don't expect to get as many approvals as you did in the past.

Despite these negative consequences, the fact remains that filing for bankruptcy can help get you out of your issues with debt. If you find yourself struggling, bankruptcy can eliminate some of your obligations to free up more income and allow you to get a fresh start. To remind you of why bankruptcy can be a good thing despite adverse consequences there are some things bankruptcy can provide for you:

- Temporarily delay or stop a foreclosure, repossession or wage garnishment.

- Prohibit debt collectors from harassing you and conducting bothersome collection activities.
- Eliminate your secured debt in exchange for your assets or give you some time to get back on track in terms of payments so that you don't have to give up your assets.
- Eliminate most of your non-priority unsecured debts.

As you can see, there are several reasons why filing for bankruptcy can be a good thing. If your only reason for hesitating is that you don't want to damage your credit score further, then you may have to reconsider your decision. There are far worse things than bankruptcy like continuing to struggle with your debt for the foreseeable future. So if you want to take a major step towards improving your quality of life, do what's right for you. Always keep your goal of living debt-free in mind and use this as your inspiration to find the best solution.

7

LIVING A DEBT-FREE LIFE IS ABOUT YOUR MINDSET

After you have addressed your debt, it's time to start thinking about your future. By applying everything you have learned in the past six chapters, you are already on your way towards paying off your debts little by little. If you stick with your budget and plan, the day will come when you make your last debt payment. Think about how you will feel on that day.

Of course, paying off your debts is just half the battle. If you want to live a debt-free life, then you need to prepare for it. As you reduce your debts, you need to ensure your financial health in the long-run by adopting new habits that will reduce or eliminate your risk of being in this position again.

127

THE IMPORTANCE OF CHANGING YOUR MINDSET

The mind is a powerful tool. If you set your mind to doing something, there is a very high likelihood that you will accomplish it. So if you don't change your current mindset along with your financial habits, there is a very high likelihood that you would start overspending and accumulating new debt in the future.

Whenever you are tempted to go back to your old spending habits, try to remember the situation you are in right now. Think about the stress you are feeling, the apprehension, and the uncertainty of your future because of the debt accumulated over the years. Hopefully, these bad memories will help bring you back to reality and remind you that you are the one in control of your financial health. After your consciousness is back on track, use these tips to keep it there:

1. When it comes to debt, only opt for "good debt."

We have already established the fact that not all debt or credit is bad. If you want to continue improving your financial health, focus your mind on good debt only. This means that when it comes to accumulating debt, only do it for things you need like medicine and food, for example. You can also take on new debt if it will improve your life in the long-run like taking out a mortgage on a home or a loan to start a business. But when it comes to luxuries or material things you want but don't need, make sure you can afford them first.

2. When using credit cards, turn off your emotional brain.

Your emotional brain usually comes into play when you find something that you really want and if you give in to it, you will end up racking up impulse purchases. Naturally, if you don't have cash-on-hand, you will need to use your credit card. Sadly, your emotional brain doesn't understand the consequences of credit card debt like finance charges or interest rates. So when you go to the mall or to any other shops that you typically buy your wants from, try turning off this side of your brain. If you can't, then try leaving your credit cards at home when navigating high risk spending areas such as these.

3. Pay your bills every month.

By this point, you would have already created an effective plan for paying your bills. Of course, your plan would include your budget. Take note of bill deadlines and keep them in the forefront of your mind during this process so as to remember them even without checking the due date. For instance, if you have three credit cards, make sure that you know each individual due date so you always make payments on time. Since you have included these debts in your budget, you should have the money to make your payments.

If you have the extra money on-hand, make your payments before they are due. Make this a habit, and when the account is paid off, shift your mindset so that the extra money you have each month goes into your savings and your emergency fund. This is a great mindset to have if you want to focus more on saving instead of spending. There are many other ways to ensure that you can pay your bills each month on time. Here are some suggestions for you:

Use credit management apps

These days, there are apps for virtually anything! Take advantage of modern technology by using reliable mobile apps to keep track of your debts to improve your credit score. Some examples of such apps are:

- **Credit Karma** where you can receive monitoring alerts for your debts. This app also comes with other helpful tools for managing your credit and you can download it for free.

- **Credit Sesame** where you can summarize your monthly payments, find out your debt balances, and monitor your credit. This free app is an excellent choice if you also have a mortgage as it offers some great tools for this purpose.

- **Debt Payoff Assistant** where you can learn more about different pay-off methods and choose the one that suits your situation best. While the main focus of this free app is the snowball method, you can opt to create your own customized plan.

- **Prism** where you can keep track of your debts by signing up all active credit cards on the app. Then it provides you with a calendar for you to see all of your paid and unpaid bills. This app is also free.

These are just some examples of the top credit management apps available for download at the time I wrote this book. You may also do your own research to find out which app would be best for you depending on your own financial situation.

Set-up automatic payments with creditors or your bank

This is a great way to ensure that your bills will be paid on-time even if you forget. Talk to your creditors about setting up automatic payments. You can do this directly with them or through your bank. For this, you would have to link one of your bank accounts to allow auto-debit payments. Just make sure that the bank account you have linked always has funds for the payments to go through automatically or additional fees can occur.

Set reminders on your smartphone's calendar

This is an easy way to remind you of your due dates. Although you would still have to make the payments manually, setting reminders will ensure that you don't forget anything. Plus, this is a very easy solution as you can just set the reminders on your smartphone in a matter of minutes.

When applying for new credit, ask if you can choose the due date for payments

Although it's not recommended to apply for new

credit while you're still struggling with debt, you can do this once you've paid off most of what you owe and you're ready to apply for new loans or credit cards. In such cases, ask your creditors or your bank if you can choose the due dates for your payments. If they agree, choose the same date for all payments so that you won't confuse what is due, when and you can easily save money to be able to make your payments in a single day.

4. Keep your goal in mind.

Finally, you can improve your mindset if you keep your goal to pay off all debts, in mind. As long as you keep telling yourself this, you will find more ways to get there. For instance, if you receive a bonus from work allocate part of that bonus (or all of it) towards your debts. But if you don't make a conscious choice to remind yourself of these debts, you might forget and just spend your bonus on things you don't need. If you really want to remind yourself of your goals, try to make them more concrete. For instance, you can:

- Create a list of your goals and either tick or cross out whenever you achieve them. The great thing about making a list is that you can easily keep track of your progress and you can even add more goals over time.

- Keep a money journal where you write down everything related to your finances. Here, you can keep track of your budget, any bonuses or extra income you've received, the payments you made, and your existing debts.

- To make things more fun and interesting, why don't you try writing your debts down on little post-it notes? Then you can even come up with a color-coding system to make it easier for you to identify your different debts. Instead of just letting your bills pile-up, create your own post-it note system where you can see your progress as you continue making payments each month. This is a creative way to show progress and stay positive!

START INVESTING

Investments are an excellent way to secure your financial future, especially when you learn how to make smart investments. Instead of spending your money on material possessions or other things that don't really add value to your life. Here are some suggestions for you in terms of investments as part of your plan to adopt healthier financial habits:

1. Build your emergency fund

It's always recommended to build an emergency fund for unexpected occurrences. That way, you can use this fund to get out of emergency situations instead of using credit cards or loans, both of which will add to your debts. Make your emergency fund part of your budget. After you have set aside money for your basic needs, your debts, and your savings, any leftover money should go into your emergency debt.

While you are still paying off your debts, you might not have a lot of money to put into your emergency fund. This is okay. You can start with small amounts as long as you remain consistent. For instance, putting $10 or $15 into your emergency fund each month will already give you $100 to $180 by the end of the year. And when you finish paying off your debts or you get any bonuses throughout the year, you can contribute to your emergency fund. Personally, I believe in utilizing an emergency fund as a backup because I have experienced being in a number of sticky situations where I had to rely on this allocated money to get out of trouble. It's always better to be prepared and once you can pay off debt (or most of them at least), you should focus on building this fund more aggressively. Here are a few steps that have worked well for me:

Set a separate goal for building your emergency fund

If you are currently overwhelmed with debt, saving up for emergencies might not seem feasible. This is the reality of your current situation and it's okay. In such a case, the best things you can do right now is set a goal for building your emergency fund. Going back to the goals you have set for paying off your debts, you can add you goals for building your emergency fund right after those goals. To make these new goals stand out, write them down using a different color. If you are printing your goals out, use a different color for these goals too. Setting your emergency fund goals will remind you to start building your emergency fund as soon as you have freed up some of your money.

To find out if you can already start working on your emergency fund goals, it's recommended to keep going back to your monthly budget and expenses. You should always keep track of all the payments you are making and all the money you are spending.

That way, you can immediately see if you have extra money to put into your emergency fund and any other savings goals you have.

Create an actionable plan so you can start saving for your emergency fund

After making a list of your goals, it's time for you to develop an actionable plan. Goal-setting and planning always go together as you cannot achieve the former without the latter. Be sure to include specific targets that are measurable for you to move towards. For instance, if your long-term emergency fund goal is to have at least $1,000 by the end of the year, you can set a target to save at least $200 to $300 each quarter for your emergency fund. Analyzing your budget and coming up with realistic amounts will provide you with the motivation you need to keep going, especially if you're able to achieve your smaller targets as you move towards your big goal.

Stick to the plan

Once you have finalized this plan, it's time to start following it. Part of your plan is to determine when you can start contributing to your emergency fund. If you don't have the funds right now, check your existing debts. If you can pay regularly, then you will have an idea of when you can pay off some of your debts completely. With this estimated date in mind, you can set a date for when you can start adding money to your emergency fund. Set a calendar reminder for it too so you won't forget.

Once you have set up your emergency fund, make sure that it is easily accessible

Finally, when your emergency fund has already been set up and you've placed money in it, make sure that you can access it easily. For instance, if you deposited the money into an account, apply for a debit card so that you can charge any expenses directly to that account. Of course, try to control yourself too if you decide to carry your debit card wherever you go. Remember that your emergency fund is only for emergencies, not for impulse shopping sprees!

Don't think of your emergency fund as another burden or obligation. Just think of it as your safety net in case you encounter an unexpected event where you need money to deal with or overcome it. If nothing bad happens to you over the years, then your emergency fund can be part of your savings or retirement fund. At the end of the day, the money you put away will still be yours. That's why you can consider this as an investment.

2. Reevaluate your goals

While you might not have the capacity to save up for these goals right now, it's always a good idea to start planning early. Even while you're still paying off your debts, you can also come up with a plan for achieving your life goals. Then when you start crossing off your debts, you can include your estimations for these goals in your budget. Apart from preset goals, you can think of other ways to enrich your financial life. If you have been struggling with debt for some time now, then you might have put everything else on hold as your money is funneled into payments. You can use this "down time" for self-reflection and get back to the basics of mental health.

Do the things that you love

While paying off your debts, you would have to set aside your hobbies and interests as you cannot really afford them. For instance, if you love collecting comic books, this involves a lot of spending. If you're deep in debt, then continuing to purchase comic books wouldn't be the most practical idea, right?

But when you have paid off your debts and you have built an adequate emergency fund, you can pick up on your curated collection of comic books that bring you happiness. Only this time, you would be more practical with how you're spending. For instance, instead of purchasing five comic books at a time, just pick the best one. More importantly, learn how to save up to sustain your hobby instead of spending your money freely even if you know that will probably bring you back to the situation you are in now.

Learning new skills to give you a competitive edge in your career

Apart from being able to finance your hobbies, getting out of debt can also enable you to move forward in your career. Therefore, another goal you may want to set for yourself would be to invest in training, workshops, and even online courses for you to learn new skills for the benefit of your profession.

For instance, if you work as a graphic designer and you have managed to pay off a few of your debts, you can sign up for online courses to help you master your craft. Think about your weaknesses and find ways to work on those. Investing in your own skills is beneficial, especially if you can use those skills to move forward in your career.

Investing in your health

Sadly, when you're stuck in a life of living from paycheck to paycheck, one of the things that takes the backseat is healthcare. After all, would you really consider paying for health insurance if you're struggling with debts and you feel fine? Probably, not.

Also, if you aren't suffering from any medical condition and you don't feel any symptoms, you probably wouldn't have yourself checked regularly. Unfortunately, if you take your health for granted, this is something you will regret in the future. Therefore, investing in your health is another goal that you might want to set for yourself. Whether it comes in the form of health insurance, regular checkups or even spa days and massages, save up to heal your body and improve your health.

Thinking about other things (or people) that matter in your life

Setting goals is all about knowing what matters to you the most. Do a bit of self-reflection to find out if anything is missing in your life. Now that you are working on your financial health, you should also think about your well-being. Do you have any projects that you have yet to start working on? Do you have any dreams that you wish you could make into reality? These are the things you can include in your goals.

If you can't think of anything for yourself, then you may start thinking about the people who matter most to you. For instance, if you have children, you may consider investing in an educational plan for them. Or if your parents are in a retirement home, you may consider moving them to one that offers better facilities. As long as you can afford to make life easier for yourself and the one you love without burying yourself in debt again, you can include these in your list of future goals.

Take some time off

Finally, you can also think of goals that allow you to take a break from your busy life. Apart from being a goal, you can also make this your reward for sticking with your debt-management plan. Once you have achieved your bigger goals (like being able to pay for one of your biggest debts), you can reward yourself with a recreational trip. You can even plan a "staycation" to give you a chance to truly relax after working hard on paying off your debts.

When setting goals, don't just think short-term. These activities will serve as your motivation to stick to the plan. Remember: slow and steady wins the race. Starting with small amounts is better than only creating plans but never taking the steps to achieve them. Saving up for achievements in life is a great investment in your future.

3. Consider making a reliable, low-risk investment for extra income

With so many ways to invest your money, it may seem like anyone can do it, so why not you? Sure, the allure of "easy money" is appealing but be aware that this also comes with high risk. Usually they say, "don't invest money you can't afford to lose," and it's a "rich man's game." Take this into consideration while still in the process of repaying your debts. Research different investment options like stocks, mutual funds, bonds or even exchange-traded funds. This way you will get a better look at money working for you, rather than the other way around. Determine which investments are right for you at a beginner level. When you have paid off your debts, you will already know where to put your money to ensure that it grows.

4. Start planning for retirement

For those who have a lot of debt, retirement is often the last thing on your mind. After all, why would you think about something that is decades away when you are dealing with financial issues now? It's okay not to think about your retirement when you're struggling with debt but when making plans for the future, include your retirement too. Again, do your research to find out which retirement options are right for you. Once you find a great retirement plan, you can apply for it and start making payments as soon as you have money freed up from paying off your debts.

LOVE YOUR JOB AND YOU WILL FIND WAYS TO EXCEL

If you want to free yourself from debt and have a good financial future, it's important to not only be employed but move up, professionally. How do you feel about your job right now? Are you happy with it or do you keep counting the hours until it's time for you to go home? If the former is true for you, keep it up! But if it's the latter, now is the time to change your perspective on this part of life. If you really want to do great work, then you must learn how to love your job. Here are some important reasons why loving your job matters:

You will feel passion

When you love your job, you will find it easier to make progress and be efficient. Passion is something felt by those doing something they enjoy, and get paid to do it. But even if you don't have the job you always dreamed of, try to appreciate your work in the little ways so you can feel better about what you do. Think about it this way: if you don't have a regular job, how else can you make money? The more passion you can find in your work, the time will fly.

Productivity will increase

When you love your work, you will be driven intrinsically. This means that you won't need external rewards or motivation to do well. Naturally, when your motivation comes from within, this will make you more productive. You'll finish your tasks faster and even without asking, you will push yourself to do more, all for the love of your work.

You will feel more positive

When you think of the people that you love, don't these thoughts make you feel more positive? In the same way, if you love your work, you will always feel more positive about it. Even when faced with challenges, you will try to find ways to overcome these challenges because you care about what you do. You know that you are making a difference in your own way, thus, you will feel happy about your job. Who knows? You might even become an inspiration to those around you!

As you can see, your love for your work will also be your driving force to excel in it. If you can do your best in your work, then you can also rely on it to provide you with a steady source of income to pay off your debts while providing your basic needs too. When it comes to employment and income generation, here are some practical tips:

- Always maintain professionalism with your colleagues and clients. This will give you an edge, especially in terms of networking leverage in the future.
- Maintain basic etiquette while at work. These include being punctual, meeting all deadlines, and doing your best when assigned new tasks.
- Make sure to keep up with your industry's

trends through research, communication or learning from the pro. The more updated you stay, the more you can contribute to your workplace making you an asset instead of a liability.

- To move forward in your work or to climb the corporate ladder, never stop learning new skills through training, workshops, and online courses. These proactive steps can increase your chances of getting promoted, and earning higher pay especially if you show you are giving it your all.

- If your income from your regular job isn't enough to cover your basic needs and debt payments, consider a side job or engaging in passive income. Just make sure that you are allowed to take part in such by going through the policies of your company. For instance, your company might have a policy that doesn't allow you to take time off for another job as long as you hold a full-time position. Or your contract might have a non-compete clause that states that you cannot work for a different company in the same industry, even if it's a different position. You must find out about these types of limitations to make sure that you're not putting your current job at risk. If needed, you can share your plans with your employer—you might even get some good ideas from them.

- If you think that there is no chance for you to move forward in your current place of work, consider looking for a better job at a different company. You don't have to settle when you know that you don't have any chance of improving your financial situation. As long as you work hard, there will always be better opportunities for you to help you achieve your debt-free life faster.

Unemployment is one of the most significant causes of debt. There's no other way around it—to pay off all your debts, you need to maintain a full-time job. Unfortunately, even your job isn't guaranteed. Many people have very little job security and it can be extremely difficult to find gainful employment even if you're highly skilled or experienced. There are plenty of opportunities to improve your job perfor-mance, by developing positive relationships with the people in your workplace, and genuinely loving your job.

KILL THE HABIT OF CREDIT CARD SPENDING

Credit card spending is the most common habit of people who are buried in debt because using credit cards is just so easy and convenient. I have already shared this tip in Chapter 4 and I am sharing it again because this is important throughout your process of debt repayment and even when you are finally debt-free. Getting rid of your credit card spending habit is one of the most important and most effective strategies to get out of—and stay out of—debt. Right now, you should only focus on paying off your debts and continuing your comfortable lifestyle by living off income. If you find something that you want to buy but doesn't fit into your budget at that moment, make a plan to save for it or forget about it. Avoid using your credit card to pay for things you can't afford unless these things are a necessity.

Only opt for balance transfers if necessary.

The only times you should opt for balance transfers are to make things simpler—like if you use a balance transfer to pay off several credit cards for consolidation—or if you use the balance transfer to pay off a credit card when there is a promotion that offers a lower interest rate. But for other reasons, balance transfers only prolong your debt and, in most cases, make them worse. After assessing your financial situation, if you think that you can pay off your debt within a given period, then you don't need to do this. It's especially important to avoid this option if it will cause you to pay more or require more time to pay off your debt.

Be aware of the telltale signs of credit card debt.

These include reaching your credit limit, using your credit card to pay for essentials, and not being able to pay more than the minimum amounts of your credit card bills. Take a moment to realize that you are already relying too much on your credit cards and if you don't stop, you will end up in debt again. This awareness should shake you out of your old habits and bring you back to the change you are trying to make. Always be aware of these telltale signs so that you can catch them early on and take the steps to get back on track.

Live within your means.

Credit cards are popular because they are extremely convenient and easy to use. When you always have access to your credit cards, you will always give in to the temptation of using them. This is why it's recommended to leave your credit cards at home, especially if you plan to go to places where you know you will be tempted to spend on things that you don't need.

Once you have gotten used to not using your credit cards all the time, you can put them back into your wallet and consciously choose not to use them. This is an important habit to learn if you want to maintain financial health. Learn how to live within your means by only spending money that you have. If you can't afford to buy things, don't. This habit will take some getting used to but if you can keep practicing it, then you can break your habit of credit card spending.

Make it a habit to pay using your debit card or cash only.

In line with the last point, you should only rely on using cash or a debit card to pay for things. In fact, you may want to consider applying for a prepaid debit card to make sure that you are only spending money that you have. Either way, only using cash or a debit card to pay for your expenses is a sure-fire way to avoid debt. With these options, you won't have to spend money that you don't have. Over time, you may even come to realize how frivolous your spending habits are and when you realize this, you will start learning how to control yourself better.

Avoid making cash advances

Swiping your credit cards to make impulse purchases is one thing but when you're stuck in a desperate situation, taking out a cash advance might be something you consider. However, cash advances are very expensive transactions as they typically come with a high-interest rate, a transaction fee, and no grace period to help you avoid paying for finance charges. Try to avoid making cash advances at all costs as these might put you in financial trouble.

There is nothing wrong with owning and using credit cards. You don't even have to close your existing credit card accounts. The key here is to learn how to use your credit cards responsibly to avoid getting buried in debts. Don't rely too much on your credit cards and you will soon learn how to depend more on the money that you actually have so you only spend on things you can afford.

SMARTER PURCHASING

Living a debt-free life doesn't mean that you have to stop buying things altogether. Even while you are paying off your debts, you can still spend your hard-earned money on things that you need and even things that you want, within reason.

Compare prices of items before purchasing.

Make it a habit to compare prices of similar items before purchasing, especially when it comes to buying high-priced items. For instance, if you need to buy a kitchen appliance, don't go for the first thing you see. Most kitchen appliances don't come cheap but you might find one that falls within your budget if you look around in different shops. The more you practice comparing prices, the more this task will come naturally to you. This habit can save you a lot of money making it an excellent step towards making smart purchasing decisions.

Stay away from "interest-free financing" or "buy now, pay later."

While these schemes may seem extremely appealing, don't buy into them right away. Even if you can take advantage of "interest-free financing" or "buy now, pay later" schemes, you would still have to pay for the purchase you made. Most of the time, these schemes are attached to luxury items or things that you don't really need. At the very least, learn more about them first before agreeing.

If you find such schemes when you're looking for something you need, then you may consider them. For instance, if you need to buy a new car and you find a dealer that offers interest-free financing, then you may consider such a deal. This is especially true if you have already looked at different shops and you haven't found any better offers. But you should also be careful of other credit card scams that might spell financial trouble for you. To help you avoid such scams, remember the following:

1. If you find an offer that's too good to be true, it probably is.
2. Check the offers for hidden charges like required contributions, high service charges or other high fees that will add to your monthly debts.
3. When dealing with credit-counseling organizations, make sure to choose one with a solid reputation. Typically, non-profit

organizations are the best ones as you won't have to pay fees to them.

Avoid making impulse purchases.

Impulse purchases are the worst as they always end up with you spending money that you don't have. To avoid impulse buying, avoid bringing large amounts of cash. Otherwise, you won't have any reason to stop yourself from buying things that you don't really need. After all, you would have the money to pay for them! It's also a good idea to make a shopping list before you go out to buy things. Whether you plan to go to the grocery store, the clothing store, the bakery or any other shop, having a list will help you shop with a purpose and avoid impulsive buying.

When you shop, follow a 50-30-20 plan.

The 50-30-20 plan was advocated by bankruptcy expert and US Senator, Elizabeth Warren. Following this plan will help you make smarter purchasing decisions as it focuses on allocating your money on important things. Let's break down this plan for you to understand it better:

1. **50%** of your money should go into your

essential expenses like food, shelter, transportation, child care, insurance, utilities, and the minimum payments of your debts. You can even use this amount for deciding whether you can afford a new debt or not. If you can still afford to pay for all of your essentials using this amount, then you can afford to take on the new debt. If not, then you should pass on the new debt you're considering.

2. **30%** of your money can go to your luxuries or your "wants." These include taking trips, eating out, and buying things that you want.
3. **20%** of your money should go into your savings, emergency funds, and investments.

It's easier to follow this plan when you create a realistic budget for your total income. If you can stick with this plan, then you can maintain your financial health for the long-run.

KEEP TRACK OF YOUR MONEY

Last but not the least, you should keep track of your money so you can see if you're working towards your financial goals or if you need to make a change.

Getting rid of debts isn't enough—you should also monitor your spending habits constantly so you can see where you can make improvements. It's time to stop your spend-now, ask-questions-later, mentality. Each purchase you make during this time should be done with careful consideration.

Since you have already made a list of debt, budget, and what you spend money on, this should be easy. Now, all you have to do is create a spreadsheet using all of the information on these lists to come up with a financial tracker for you to keep track of your money. This kind of document can benefit you a lot as you can also see your own spending trends and patterns. As you update this spreadsheet, you can determine whether your spending habits are helping you move towards your financial goals or not. For the latter, you should start taking the necessary steps to get back on track.

This strategy is especially important while you are still in the process of paying off your debts. But even when you have paid them off, continue to keep track of your money so you can continue with your good habits by constantly making improvements to them. Making any kind of significant change in your life involves awareness and conscious effort.

You can do this in different ways. If a financial tracking spreadsheet isn't for you, there are apps you can download for the same purpose. You can even come up with your own system of monitoring your finances to ensure that you understand the system and you can customize it as needed. Just keep going until the good habits have become part of your life and you can confidently say that you have your finances totally under control.

The Beauty of Living Debt-Free

Living a debt-free life is within your grasp... All you have to do is take the necessary steps to eliminate your debts to improve your financial health.

From the beginning of this eBook, you have learned everything you need to start taking this journey. We started by helping you realize the reality of your situation. As with any other big change, you must first accept that you have a problem before you can work on solving it. To do this, you must assess your own financial situation, learn everything that you can about it, and understand how you can keep track of your finances to ensure that you don't get stuck in the future. This is why I wanted the first chapter to focus on learning how to calculate your DTI, finding out what a reasonable amount of debt is, and knowing the signs that you are already in trouble with debt. When you know all of these things, you will truly be able to understand your current financial situation.

In the next chapter, we went through the most common—and most dangerous—myths people believe about credit and debt. If you are currently struggling with debt, chances are, you believed these myths which, in turn, might have contributed to the situation you are in. But now that you know the truth, it should be easier for you to make wiser decisions in terms of your finances. Gone are the days when you would feel apprehensive because you have always believed certain things about debts which, as it turns out, aren't really true. After reading this chapter, things should have been clearer for you, thus, allowing you to do what's necessary to start getting rid of your debts.

We then took a quick look at some of the more uncommon strategies before discussing the most common and most effective ones. After you analyze your own financial situation, then you can choose which strategy to use. Then we moved on to practical, simple, and effective strategies to help you build healthier money-spending habits. After that, the next thing we tackled were the most common issues that come with having a lot of debt. After explaining these issues, I had shared some practical ways to deal with them in case you might encounter such as you work to eliminate your debts.

Throughout the different chapters, one thing that came up frequently was bankruptcy. This is definitely significant as it could be your last resort for a number of situations. Understanding bankruptcy is important so you know when to file for it and whether it is the best option for you to take. Finally, the last chapter rounded everything off as it focused on some killer strategies to help you eliminate debt and secure a bright financial future for yourself. As promised, I have provided you with everything you need to live a debt-free life. I've shared all the fundamental information you would need to heal your financial health and maintain it for the rest of your life.

It will take a lot of effort and time but as I have seen from the clients I've worked with in the past, getting rid of debts and creating healthier financial habits is completely doable. Thank you very much for reading my eBook all the way to the end and I sincerely hope that you can apply everything you have learned to turn your financial situation around and remove one important stressor from your life. If you believe that this book has helped you out as I hope it had, you could leave a positive review so that other people in the same position can also start improving their lives. Good luck with your journey and keep motivating yourself to move forward until your life is completely free of debts!

REFERENCES

11 Credit Myths: Don't Fall for 'Em. (2018). Retrieved from https://www.experian.com/blogs/ask-experian/11-credit-myths-dont-fall-for-em/

Bankruptcy and Debt Collectors. (2011). Retrieved from https://consumerlawyer.mn/bankruptcy-and-debt-collectors/

Bieber, C. (2019). Here's How Much Debt the Average American Had in 2018. Retrieved from https://www.fool.com/personal-finance/2019/05/14/how-much-debt-average-american-had-in-2018.aspx

Chen, J. (2019). Learn about Debt. Retrieved from https://www.investopedia.com/terms/d/debt.asp

Chorpenning, A. (2019). What Is the Snowball Method? How to Use It to Pay off Debt. Retrieved from https://www.creditkarma.com/advice/i/what-is-the-snowball-method/

Confucius. (n.d.). It doesn't matter how slow you go, as long as you do not stop - Confucius. Retrieved from https://www.plurk.com/p/gwrmir

Credit and Debt: Good vs. Bad Credit. (n.d.). Retrieved from https://www.smartaboutmoney.org/Courses/Money-Basics/Credit-and-Debt/Good-vs-Bad-Credit

Davis, S. (2019). Credit Repair: How To Fix Bad Credit On Your Own In 6 Steps. Retrieved from https://www.moneyunder30.com/credit-repair

Debt Consolidation - How to Consolidate Your Debt. (n.d.). Retrieved from https://www.debt.org/consolidation/

Debt-to-Income Ratio: How to Calculate Your DTI. (2019). Retrieved from https://www.nerdwallet.com/article/loans/personal-loans/calculate-debt-income-ratio

Delbridge, E. (2020). If You Are Thinking of Hiding Your Car From the Repo Man, Think Again.

Retrieved from https://www.thebalance.com/does-hiding-a-car-to-avoid-repossession-actually-work-527154

Fay, B. (n.d.). Consumer Debt Statistics & Demographics in America. Retrieved from https://www.debt.org/faqs/americans-in-debt/demographics/

Fay, B. (n.d.). Debt Myths - Common Debt, Credit and Bankruptcy Misconceptions. Retrieved from https://www.debt.org/advice/myths/

Fay, B. (n.d.). Debt Snowball Method Works - But It Will Cost You $$$$. Retrieved from https://www.debt.org/advice/debt-snowball-method-how-it-works/

Fay, B. (n.d.). Advice on How to Keep Yourself out of Debt. Retrieved from https://www.debt.org/advice/avoiding-debt/

Fay, B. (2019). Understanding Bankruptcy: How to File & Qualifications. Retrieved from https://www.debt.org/bankruptcy/

Harkness , B. (2020). How to Pay Off Debt: 6 Strategies That Work. Retrieved from https://www.creditcardinsider.com/learn/reducing-debt/

Haynes, D. (2019). What Is Bankruptcy? Retrieved

from   https://www.thebalance.com/what-is-bankruptcy-316134

Higuera, V. (2019). 6 Signs That You're Carrying Too Much Debt. Retrieved from https://www.moneycrashers.com/signs-too-much-debt/

How a Debt Management Plan Affects Your Credit: Pros & Cons. (2019). Retrieved from https://credit.org/2012/05/25/how-a-debt-management-plan-affects-your-credit/

How Creditors Collect Debts: Repossession, Wage Garnishment, Bank Attachment, and More. (n.d.). Retrieved from https://www.nolo.com/legal-encyclopedia/debt-collection-repossessions-wage-garnishments-property-levies-more

How to Stop Debt Collector Harassment. (2018). Retrieved from https://bankruptcy.findlaw.com/debt-relief/how-to-stop-debt-collector-harassment.html

Irby, L. T. (2020). 4 Must-Have Apps for Managing Your Credit. Retrieved from https://www.thebalance.com/mobile-apps-for-managing-credit-960096

Irby, L. T. (2019). 10 Strategies for Paying Off Your

Debt. Retrieved from https://www.thebalance.com/start-getting-out-of-debt-960852

Irby, L. T. (2019). Should You Follow the 20/10 Rule for Debt Management? Retrieved from https://www.thebalance.com/should-you-follow-the-20-10-rule-for-debt-management-4164476

Irby, L. T. (2019). Here Are 10 Signs You Have Too Much Debt. Retrieved from https://www.thebalance.com/signs-you-have-too-much-debt-960865

Irby, L. T. (2019). 6 Reasons You Shouldn't Use Your Credit Card in an Emergency. Retrieved from https://www.thebalance.com/why-using-your-credit-card-for-emergencies-is-risky-960992

Irby, L. T. (2019). 12 Common Debt Collectors Myths Debunked. Retrieved from https://www.thebalance.com/myths-about-debt-collectors-4046409

Irby, L. T. (2020). A Simple Explanation of Debt Consolidation. Retrieved from https://www.thebalance.com/what-you-must-know-about-debt-consolidation-960652

Irby, L. T. (2020). Following These 10 Steps Will

Help Avoid Creating Credit Card Debt. Retrieved from https://www.thebalance.com/avoid-credit-card-debt-960043

Irby, L. T. (2020). What to Do If You Can't Make Your Minimum Credit Card Payments. Retrieved from https://www.thebalance.com/cant-make-minimum-credit-card-payment-961000

Irby, L. T. (2019). Your Debt-To-Income Ratio, and How to Calculate It. Retrieved from https://www.thebalance.com/how-to-calculate-your-debt-to-income-ratio-960851

Jaggernath, J. (n.d.). 5 Myths About Debt Payments – Fact versus Fiction. Retrieved from https://www.nomoredebts.org/blog/dealing-with-debt/5-myths-about-debt-payments-fact-versus-fiction

Jaggernath, J. (n.d.). 4 Credit Card Minimum Payment Myths & How to Avoid the Pitfalls: My Money Coach. Retrieved from https://www.mymoneycoach.ca/blog/4-credit-card-minimum-payment-myths-how-to-avoid-pitfalls

Johnson, H. (2019). 11 Ways to Get Out of Debt Faster. Retrieved from https://www.thesimpledollar.com/credit/manage-debt/11-ways-to-get-out-of-debt-faster/

Joy, D. (n.d.). How Much Debt Is Too Much: Signs You Have Too Much Credit Card Debt. Retrieved from https://www.incharge.org/debt-relief/how-much-debt-is-too-much/

Kagan, J. (2019). Parsing the 28/36 Rule. Retrieved from https://www.investopedia.com/terms/t/twenty-eight-thirty-six-rule.asp

Kagan, J. (2020). Debt Consolidation. Retrieved from https://www.investopedia.com/terms/d/debtconsolidation.asp

Lane, S. (2012). Options to Avoid Car Repossession. Retrieved from https://www.nolo.com/legal-encyclopedia/options-avoid-car-repossession.html

Lane, S. (2019). Stopping Wage Garnishment Without Bankruptcy. Retrieved from https://www.alllaw.com/articles/nolo/bankruptcy/stopping-wage-garnishment-without-bankruptcy.html

Law Offices of Marji Hanson. (n.d.). Retrieved from https://www.utahbklaw.com/bankruptcy-solutions/benefits-of-bankruptcy/eliminate-debt-stop-foreclosure/

Lee, J., & Pyles, S. (2019). 7 Tips to Pay Off Debt - From Those Who Succeeded. Retrieved from https://www.nerdwallet.com/blog/finance/7-tips-for-paying-off-debt-from-people-who-did-it/

Leonhardt, M. (2019). Americans have $29,000 in debt-and many say they'll be paying it off forever. Retrieved from https://www.cnbc.com/2019/09/19/americans-dont-know-when-theyll-pay-off-their-debt.html

Liking Your Job Helps You Succeed. (2018). Retrieved from https://appliedpsychologydegree.usc.edu/blog/how-liking-your-job-will-help-you-succeed/

Lockert, M. (2019). What's Next? A Guide to Setting Long-Term Goals After Paying Off Debt. Retrieved from https://investorjunkie.com/budgeting/longterm-goals-paying-debt/

Loftsgordon, A. (2020). Last Minute Strategies to Stop Foreclosure. Retrieved from https://www.nolo.com/legal-encyclopedia/last-minute-strategies-stop-foreclosure.html

Mastroeni, T. (2018). Facing Foreclosure? Here Are 5 Things You Can Do To Slow Down The Process. Retrieved from https://www.forbes.com/sites/taramastroeni/2018/08/23/facing-foreclosure-here-are-5-things-you-can-do-to-slow-down-the-process/#78ab44d46a6d

Matthews, K. (2014). 10 Priorities You Should Re-Evaluate to Live a Happier Life. Retrieved from https://www.startofhappiness.com/10-overlooked-priorities-re-evaluate-live-happier-life/

Michalos, H. (2019). A Complete Guide to Joint Debts. Retrieved from https://www.hoyes.com/blog/a-complete-guide-to-joint-debts/

Michon, K. (2019). Using Chapter 7 Bankruptcy to Stop Wage Garnishment. Retrieved from https://www.alllaw.com/articles/nolo/bankruptcy/chapter-7-stop-wage-garnishment.html

Mourdoukoutas, P. (2012). Why we Accumulate Bad Personal Debt? Retrieved from https://www.forbes.com/sites/panosmourdoukoutas/2012/03/31/why-we-accumulate-bad-personal-debt/

Muniz, K. (2014). How to Know When Bankruptcy Is Your Best Option. Retrieved from https://www.fool.com/investing/general/2014/01/26/how-to-know-when-bankruptcy-is-your-best-option.aspx

O'Neill, C. (2013). What Bankruptcy Can and Cannot Do. Retrieved from https://www.nolo.com/

legal-encyclopedia/chapter-7-13-bankruptcy-limits-benefits-30025.html

O'Shea, B., & Pyles, S. (2019). How to Use Debt Snowball to Pay Off Debt. Retrieved from https://www.nerdwallet.com/blog/finance/what-is-a-debt-snowball/

O'Shea, B., & Pyles, S. (2019). Debt avalanche or debt snowball, what's your type? Retrieved from https://www.nerdwallet.com/blog/finance/what-is-a-debt-avalanche/

Pangestu, D. (n.d.). Is Bankruptcy My Best Option? Retrieved from https://www.nomoredebts.org/blog/bankruptcy/when-declaring-bankruptcy-not-right-for-you

Papandrea, D. (2019). 5 Credit Card Management Apps to Stay on Top of Payments. Retrieved from https://creditcards.usnews.com/articles/credit-card-management-apps-to-stay-on-top-of-payments

Picardo, E. (2018). What Is a Reasonable Amount of Debt? Retrieved from https://www.investopedia.com/ask/answers/12/reasonable-amount-of-debt.asp

Potter, C. (2019). Will Your Partner's Debts Affect You? Retrieved from https://www.payplan.com/blog/will-partners-debts-affect/

Pritchard, J. (2019). Eliminate Debt and Minimize Interest Costs With a Debt Avalanche. Retrieved from https://www.thebalance.com/get-out-of-debt-with-debt-avalanche-4140758

Pyles, S. (2019). What Is Debt and How to Handle It. Retrieved from https://www.nerdwallet.com/blog/finance/debt/

Pyles, S. (2020). 5 Bankruptcy Facts. Retrieved from https://www.nerdwallet.com/blog/finance/5-bankruptcy-myths-dispelled/

Reasons to Do What You Love for a Living. (2017). Retrieved from https://www.businessnewsdaily.com/7995-reasons-to-do-what-you-love.html

Silverman, J., & Grabianowski, E. (2005). How Bankruptcy Works. Retrieved from https://money.howstuffworks.com/personal-finance/debt-management/bankruptcy1.htm

Smith, A. (2020). 9 Ways to Pay Off Debt. Retrieved from https://www.fool.com/the-ascent/credit-cards/articles/9-ways-to-pay-off-debt/

Start an Emergency Fund. (n.d.). Retrieved from https://www.saveandinvest.org/military-everyday-finances/start-emergency-fund

Steinberg , S., & Snider, S. (2019). 10 Easy Ways to Pay Off Debt. Retrieved from https://money.usnews.com/money/personal-finance/debt/articles/easy-ways-to-pay-off-debt

Tardi, C. (2019). What's a Debt Avalanche? Retrieved from https://www.investopedia.com/terms/d/debt-avalanche.asp

Tips for Avoiding Debt. (2018). Retrieved from https://bankruptcy.findlaw.com/debt-relief/tips-for-avoiding-debt.html

Turner, K. (2019). Every Type of Bankruptcy Explained. Retrieved from https://upsolve.org/learn/every-type-of-bankruptcy-explained/

Turner, K. (2020). How Can I Stop My Wages From Being Garnished? Retrieved from https://upsolve.org/learn/stop-wage-garnishment/

Types of Bankruptcy - Chapter 7 vs. Chapter 13. (2019). Retrieved from https://www.greenpath.com/types-of-bankruptcy/

Vohwinkle, J. (2019). These 10 Warning Signs Could

Indicate You're in Over Your Head on Debt. Retrieved from https://www.thebalance.com/warning-signs-too-much-debt-1289639

Wait, R. (2013). 10 most common debt myths. Retrieved from https://www.moneysupermarket.com/money-made-easy/ten-most-common-debt-myths/

Weintraub, E. (2019). How to Save Your Home From Foreclosure. Retrieved from https://www.thebalance.com/best-ways-to-stop-a-foreclosure-1798169

Weston, L. (2020). When Bankruptcy Is the Best Option. Retrieved from https://www.nerdwallet.com/blog/finance/bankruptcy-best-option/

What Are the Types of Bankruptcies? (2020). Retrieved from https://www.daveramsey.com/blog/types-of-bankruptcies

What is a debt-to-income ratio? Why is the 43% debt-to-income ratio important? (2019). Retrieved from https://www.consumerfinance.gov/ask-cfpb/what-is-a-debt-to-income-ratio-why-is-the-43-debt-to-income-ratio-important-en-1791/

Made in the USA
Monee, IL
02 July 2020

35612148R00104